TRAVEL

BRITTANY

WITHDRAWN

By
El

Written by Elisabeth Morris, updated by Julian Rogers
Original photography by Rick Strange

Essex County Council Libraries

Published by Thomas Cook Publishing
A division of Thomas Cook Tour Operations Limited.
Company registration no. 1450464 England
The Thomas Cook Business Park, Unit 9, Coningsby Road,
Peterborough PE3 8SB, United Kingdom
Email: books@thomascook.com, Tel: + 44 (0) 1733 416477
www.thomascookpublishing.com

Produced by Cambridge Publishing Management Limited
Burr Elm Court, Main Street, Caldecote CB23 7NU

ISBN: 978-1-84848-069-8

© 2002, 2005, 2007 Thomas Cook Publishing
This fourth edition © 2009
Text © Thomas Cook Publishing
Maps © Thomas Cook Publishing

Series Editor: Maisie Fitzpatrick
Project Editor: Linda Bass
Production/DTP: Steven Collins

Printed and bound in Italy by Printer Trento

Cover photography: Front L–R: © Spila Riccardo/4Corners Images;
© Richard Wayman/Alamy; © Stefano Amantini/4Corners Images.
Back: © Fantuz Olimpio/4Corners Images.

The paper used for this book has been independently certified as having
been sourced from well-managed forests and other controlled sources
according to the rules of the Forest Stewardship Council.
This book has been printed and bound in Italy by Printer Trento S.r.l.,
an FSC certified company for printing books on FSC mixed paper in
compliance with the chain of custody and on products labelling standards.

FSC

Mixed Sources
Product group from well-managed
forests and other controlled sources

Cert no. CQ-COC-000012
www.fsc.org
© 1996 Forest Stewardship Council

Contents

KEY TO MAPS

▲ 320m	Mountain	★	Start of walk/tour
〬	Ancient walls	★	Start of walk/tour
[i]	Information	N171	Road number
■	POI	☸	Viewpoint

Introduction

Jutting out into the Atlantic Ocean on the western edge of the European continent, Brittany is a part of France with unique appeal.

'The Bretons are born with seawater round the eyes, and the ocean flows through their veins.'

Local Proverb

You may have heard about Brittany from an enthusiastic friend or seen an enticing travel programme or brochure, and the name keeps turning up every time you think of holidays ahead. Colour shots flash through your mind: of rocks in a cloud of sea spray, of white sails on an emerald sea, of golden sand and shellfish, of friendly quayside cafés. But you still ask yourself, 'Is it really for me? What kind of holiday can I expect?'

The key word is variety – and there is certainly enough of it in every sense.

Brittany

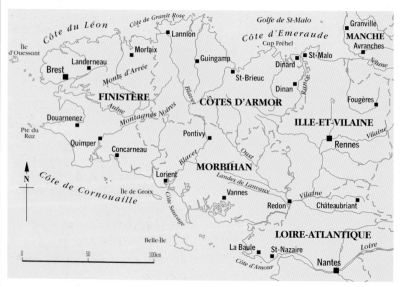

Introduction

The two faces of Brittany

The landscape of Brittany is literally defined by its contrasts. 'Armor' (literally 'land of the sea') is the coastal fringe, its varied contours characterised by working harbours, seaside resorts, long stretches of wild, uninhabited shoreline, islands and cliffs teeming with birds. 'Argoat' (the 'land of the woods') is the other green, inland Brittany, with its fields and forests, rivers, mountains and moors.

The sea, the scudding clouds and the omnipresent granite blend their greys and greens into a subtle yet powerfully attractive picture. Westerly winds – responsible for the changing moods of the sky – sweep vigorously over the land, ensuring summer temperatures that rarely soar.

A land of traditions

The Bretons are a seafaring people with deep religious convictions. Megaliths, castles, parish closes and calvaries are fascinating reminders that their culture is steeped in both paganism and Christianity. Their ancestral language, music and costumes live on in the numerous festivals that take place in delightful old cities.

A holidaymakers' paradise

Whether you have an interest in fine food and drink, archaeology, fishing, church art, sunbathing, domestic architecture of the Middle Ages, birdwatching, castles or canoeing – or

The polders around Dol-de-Bretagne: the former marshlands are now cut with canals and farmed

in all of the above, and more – you'll find an opportunity in Brittany to pursue it.

You can drive through constantly changing scenery, walk through forests and across moors, cruise its rivers and cycle along canals. Relax on sheltered sandy beaches, sail round the islands, have a game of golf or take the children to a water park.

Also included in this book are the lower reaches of the River Loire so as to include Nantes, the former capital of Brittany.

The land

Covering an area of some 30,000sq km (11,500sq miles), the Breton Peninsula has arrived at its present shape after aeons of interaction between earth and elements. Its mountains were formed in the Primary Period. Around 600 million years ago, its granite was slowly eroded to its present height of less than 400m (1,312ft).

A sudden rise in sea level during the Quaternary Period, which began a mere 2 million years ago, caused low-lying areas to be flooded: river valleys became *abers* (shallow estuaries), a distinctive feature of the jagged west coast, while hilltops became the numerous islands surrounding the peninsula.

Temperate climate

With the warming influence of the Gulf Stream, winter is mild and temperatures stay above freezing, but storms can be spectacular in places such as the Pointe du Raz on the Atlantic coast. Spring is a busy time on the wildlife front, as the return of the warm weather brings intense activity in the numerous bird colonies, and the sudden blossoming of gorse all over the countryside.

In summer, temperatures average 18°C (64°F) and, although the weather is sometimes unpredictable, the sun is never far away and shines generously on the beaches. While autumn lingers on peacefully inland, the sea starts to show signs of restlessness, heralding winter storms.

Abundant nature

The constant struggle between sea and land has resulted in 2,500km (1,554 miles) of deeply indented coastline, with marked contrasts between the north, west and south coasts. The ruggedness of the northern

Granite boulders, near Le Castel

coastline is tempered by the unusual pink rock formations of the Côte de Granit Rose. To the west, taking the brunt of the onslaught of the mighty Atlantic, the coast of Finistère is austere, with dark sombre cliffs like those of the Crozon Peninsula. The sunny south coast stretches its long sandy beaches from Le Pouldu to La Baule.

All round the coast, from Bréhat in the north to Belle-Île in the south, the islands reflect the diversity of the mainland: large or small, fertile or barren, each has its own charm. Life along the coast is regulated by tidal movements which leave enormous areas uncovered and boats stranded. It is an absorbing pastime to gather shellfish at low tide, but it's wise to follow a timetable of the tides to avoid getting caught by rapidly rising waters.

Extending from the Île d'Ouessant to the Monts d'Arrée, the Parc Naturel Régional d'Armorique creates a link between coastal and inland Brittany. Once entirely covered with dense forests, the undulating countryside offers a pleasing patchwork of fields separated by low stone walls, austere mountains, moors, rivers and lakes.

Tranquil waters wash the jagged teeth of the coastline off Pointe St-Mathieu

quantities. Inland, apple orchards alternate with cornfields and pastures, with dairy produce and pork still forming a large proportion of agricultural production. The hard work needed to make a living on the land has forced countless generations of Bretons to rely on the wealth of the sea. Hence, farmers are often fishermen as well, although fishing is less lucrative than it used to be. The sea also provides a natural fertiliser in the form of *goémon*, a species of seaweed gathered at low tide.

Expanding economy

Improved communications have pulled Brittany out of its long isolation, and decentralisation has given a boost to the region's economy. Poultry-farming is booming, and fish-farming and seaweed-farming also have a bright future. Although the food and car industries are doing well, the main fields of expansion are electronics, telecommunications, service industries, research and tourism.

Poor land

Agriculture has always been important, although the land is generally poor – except along the coast, where the early vegetables of the Ceinture Dorée (Golden Belt) are grown in great

History

5000–2000 BC	Brittany's first known inhabitants, of obscure origin, erect the megaliths.
6th century BC	Arrival of the Celts. They call their new country Armor (land by the sea). Their society is well structured and they are skilled craftsmen and seafarers.
56 BC	The most powerful Celtic tribe, the Veneti from the region of Vannes, is defeated by Caesar in a sea battle off the Rhuys Peninsula.
56 BC– AD 350	The Roman occupation of Gallia Armorica brings peace, a new language (Latin) and a new religion (Christianity).
460	Massive immigration of more Celts from across the Channel, as they flee invading hordes of Angles and Saxons. They give Armorique a new name, Petite Bretagne (Little Britain), and rekindle the native population's religious fervour. The parish (*plou*) becomes the basic social and administrative unit throughout the country.
9th century	The Breton chief, Nominoë, becomes the first Duke of Brittany. In 845 Nominoë defeats his suzerain, the King of the Franks, and his son, Erispoë, becomes King of Brittany.
10th century	The Duke of Brittany, Alain Barbe-Torte ('Twisted Beard'), puts an end to Viking raids and chooses Nantes as his capital. After the death of Alain Barbe-Torte, the feudal lords defy the authority of the Duke of Brittany, who is forced to acknowledge the King of France as his suzerain.
1341	The War of Succession begins, and the bitter conflict between France and England – both countries supporting contenders to the Duchy of Brittany – is brought to a head.
1364	The French contender, Charles de Blois, is defeated and killed at the Battle of Auray, which marks the end of the civil war. The

English contender, Jean de Montfort, becomes Duke of Brittany.

1381	Jean de Montfort swears allegiance to the French king.
15th century	The economic and cultural Golden Age of the Duchy of Brittany.
1488	Duke François II, leading a coalition against the French king, is defeated at the Battle of St-Aubin-du-Cormier and dies shortly afterwards, leaving the duchy to his 12-year-old daughter, Anne.
1491	In order to end the conflict between France and Brittany, Anne marries the King of France, Charles VIII.
1499	After the death of Charles VIII, Anne marries the new King of France, Louis XII, who grants Brittany a certain amount of autonomy.
1514	Anne's daughter Claude marries the future King of France, François I, and gives him the Duchy of Brittany.
1532	After Claude's death, François I persuades the Breton parliament to ratify the Treaty of Union between France and Brittany, allowing the new province to keep some of its former independence.
1598	The Edict of Nantes, ending religious strife between Catholics and Protestants which has torn France apart since 1562, is signed by the King of France, Henri IV.
17th & 18th centuries	Relations between France and Brittany are often stormy, mainly over the issue of excessive taxation. The economy, however, prospers.
1660–1715	Reign of Louis XIV, the Sun King.
14 July 1789	Start of the French Revolution with the storming of the Bastille.

Jean de Montfort, Duke of Brittany

1793–1804	The royalist Chouans lead Brittany into a guerilla-style war against the new French Republic. Their chief, Georges Cadoudal, is executed.
19th century	The slow economic decline of Brittany prompts the birth of nationalist movements.
1940–45	The Breton people give wholehearted support to the Resistance movement. The postwar years are marked by an economic and cultural revival.
1962	First television link by satellite from Pleumeur-Bodou.
1966	Inauguration of the Rance estuary tidal power station.
1969	Small, disparate terrorist groups put forward demands for an independent Brittany.
1969–70	Creation of the Armorique and Brière Regional Nature Parks.
1975	The search for oil begins.
1977	Diwan schools (where lessons are taught in the Breton language) are created.
1985	Road signs throughout Brittany become bilingual (Breton/French).
1996	The pope visits Brittany to take part in the pilgrimage of Ste Anne.
1999	The *Erika* sinks, bringing disastrous oil slicks to Brittany's coast.
2000	The Brittany Revolutionary Army is blamed for planting a bomb in a Prevert McDonald's which kills one member of staff.
2000	TV Breizh, the first all-Breton language TV station, is launched.
2001	Diwan schools are given full government grants.
2005	France votes *non* to ratify the European Union constitutional treaty, but most Breton voters support it.
2008	First French hydro-power turbine installed in the estuary of the Odette River.

Politics

When the Act of Union was signed in 1532, Brittany became a French province, relinquishing all forms of autonomy and accepting policy decisions taken by the government in Paris. Because this system proved detrimental to the region's economic development, the nationalist movement's popularity grew alongside general discontent until, in the 1980s, the regions were given increased economic responsibilities, which led to rapid modernisation. This policy is gradually showing positive results.

Central government

France is a republic and Paris is the seat of government, comprising Parliament, the President and the Government. Parliament consists of the National Assembly, elected for five years, which votes on the laws, and the Senate, elected for nine years, which proposes amendments.

The president of the Republic, elected for seven years, chooses the prime minister from the party that holds the majority in the National Assembly.

The president is chief of the armed forces and conducts foreign affairs jointly with the government, headed by the prime minister, assisted by a variable number of ministers. The government is answerable to the National Assembly.

There are several political parties, representing the whole spectrum of opinions from left to right.

Local government

Brittany is administered by a Regional Council based in Rennes, which has the authority to take limited decisions in the fields of economic development, communications, education and culture.

As in the rest of France, the region is divided into *départements*, each of which is run by a General Council based in the principal town (in brackets).

The four *départements* of Brittany are: Ille-et-Vilaine (Rennes), Côtes d'Armor (St-Brieuc), Finistère (Quimper) and Morbihan (Vannes).

THE BRETON FLAG AND THE *TRISKELL*

The Breton flag was officially used for the first time in 1925, yet its symbolic meaning recalls Brittany's ancient history. The black and white stripes represent the nine original Breton bishoprics, while the ermine in the top left-hand corner is the heraldic symbol of the Duchy of Brittany.

The *triskell* is a decorative motif of Celtic origin found on ancient jewellery and coins throughout Europe and on Irish medieval manuscripts. Today, it is regarded as a symbol of Celtic identity.

The Celts

Brittany is today one of the last Celtic bastions of Western Europe. At a time when the making of Europe has focused public attention on cultural specificity, Brittany emerges as one of the cornerstones of European identity. Thus, the dream of a cultural awakening, nurtured by many Bretons since the 19th century, is being revived, and numerous associations and Celtic circles, encouraged by the Institut Culturel de Bretagne, do their utmost to preserve Brittany's Celtic heritage.

Gauls and Bretons

The Celtic invasions which took place around the 6th century BC are traditionally considered as having laid the foundations of the French nation, since the Celts spread and prospered over the whole territory of what is now France and became known as Gaul. The desperate struggle of the Gauls against Caesar's legions is a subject of national pride from which has sprung the heroes of one of the most successful French cartoons – *Astérix*, translated into many languages. In the 5th century AD, Brittany received a second wave of Celts from across the Channel.

Known as Bretons, they helped to reinforce the Celtic cultural impact on the whole region, which was both spiritual and material.

The Celtic heritage

When they settled in Brittany, the Celts readily absorbed the civilisation of the megaliths which had preceded them, while theirs denoted a highly original combination of myth and reality.

Their well-structured society reached its peak during the La Tène period between the 5th and 1st centuries BC. The Druids,

Calvaire, Plovan

Gauguin's *Breton Peasant Women* (see pp102–3)

who were high-ranking members of this society, were in charge of religion, and, to a great extent, of justice and education; poetic myths and legends played an important role in their teachings, and they conducted religious services in clearings in the forest. Human sacrifices were common practice.

Five powerful tribes occupied Brittany, including the Veneti in the south, whose ships boldly ventured on trading expeditions to the Mediterranean and to the British Isles.

But the Celts were above all farmers and clever craftsmen with a highly developed aesthetic sense, who shared a common language and artistic traditions with other Celtic countries, in particular Britain. Similarities in decoration have been found on ceramics on both sides of the Channel, for instance, the palm leaf of Greek origin; and on metal objects, a Celtic speciality, decorated with a great variety of original motifs and symbols such as the *triskell* (see p11). The Musée des Beaux-Arts in Rennes and the Musée d'Archéologie Régionale in Nantes both have interesting collections of regional Celtic art.

Culture

The strength and specificity of Breton culture lies in the people's awareness of their past and in their will to maintain continuity, while accepting the challenge of changing economic and social conditions. This apparent contradiction stems both from the Breton temperament and from Brittany's geographical and historical context.

The highly individualistic and proud Bretons lived for centuries in voluntary isolation until well after Brittany was officially united with France. Later on, centralised economic policies and an inadequate communications network continued to keep Brittany in relative isolation until after World War II.

This context was detrimental to the economic life of the region, but at the same time it ensured the survival of the Celtic language and of a wealth of traditions, which today still form part of the Breton way of life. The sense of isolation also encouraged a highly original form of religious art to flourish.

Daily life

To an outsider, daily life in Brittany appears very much the same as in any other region of France, and, unless you arrive on the day a *pardon* or folk festival is taking place, you might well wonder what is so special about Brittany.

The same contrast exists between town and country as anywhere in France: two-thirds of the population now live in towns, and the number of jobs available in commerce, administration and the service industries has tripled since the 1950s, a familiar trend throughout the country. Town centres are lively, with colourful markets, elegant shops, and enticing restaurants, while the countryside is deeply marked by traditional farming activities, still archaic in places.

The sea, however, is an element of daily life more omnipresent in Brittany than in other French regions: it epitomises the Breton spirit of independence, and, to many youngsters, going to sea is still an obsession.

The Bretons are, of course, very much a part of the French nation (although some nationalist extremists might disagree), and they bear certain characteristics, such as an individualistic temperament or a sense

Culture

of hospitality, which foreigners promptly recognise.

But there are subtle differences between French people from various regions. The Bretons, for instance, are known for their changing moods: they can sometimes be uncommunicative and at other times enthusiastic; they also have a vivid imagination and a definite inclination towards fantastic stories and the supernatural.

Traditions

Having always felt the need to assert their cultural identity, the Bretons have jealously guarded their traditions which are today kept alive through folk festivals and colourful pageants steeped in Celtic culture, in which music, dance and costumes are the essential ingredients, together with sporting contests and traditional games similar to those practised in other Celtic regions such as Cornwall and Scotland. Still very prominent in Breton life, religion also has its typical celebrations called *pardons*, which attract mixed crowds of believers and tourists (*see pp158–9*).

Costumes and *coiffes*

The best celebrations are marked by special clothing, and folk festivals and *pardons* are no exception. The amazing variety of traditional dress is due to the fact that, in the past, each parish had its distinctive costume and lacy headdress (*coiffe*) which female parishioners wore for Mass on Sunday, for family

THOMAS COOK'S BRITTANY

Thomas Cook introduced excursions to Brittany as early as 1865. However, they aroused little interest until the 1880s; this was ascribed to the lack of a railway network, which was late to develop in the region.

This situation lingered, and even a decade later, Cook's own guidebook to the area mentioned (ironically as an advantage) the continuing scarcity of British visitors to the region.

By the turn of the century, however, tours of Brittany had caught on. Dinard, in particular, had become a highly popular favourite with Cook's customers.

gatherings and for collective festive occasions. Nowadays, apart from festivals, *coiffes* are rarely seen except on some older women on Sundays.

The best-known costumes are from Cornouaille, where traditions have their strongest adherents. The main components of women's costumes are dresses, often black but richly embroidered; aprons covering the

A Breton *coiffe*

A satisfying camaraderie characterises the life of these fishermen at Dahouët port, Le Val-André

greater part of the dress fronts and elaborately decorated with lace and embroidered motifs; and, above all, *coiffes*, delicate like butterfly wings in Pont-Aven or rigid and rising high above the head in Bigouden country.

Men's costumes include embroidered waistcoats, short black jackets and large-brimmed felt hats with a shiny buckle and long ribbons floating in the breeze.

The Breton language

Breton is still widely spoken, particularly in the western part of the region known as the Basse Bretagne. Closely related to Welsh, it is the only Celtic language spoken on the European mainland, and today it is taught in schools and at universities, while great efforts are made to promote its use among the native population through literature, radio broadcasts and television programmes.

Breton arts and crafts

Breton art found its most original expression in village churches and parish closes (*see pp98–9*), which bear witness to the religious fervour, bold

imagination and artistic sense of the Breton people. There is a wealth of *musées des arts et traditions populaires* (crafts and traditions museums) where it is possible to admire Quimper pottery, delicate lace and carved oak furniture: in particular, *lits clos*, beds enclosed within elaborately decorated cupboards as a protection against the cold.

Saints and legends

To the Bretons, the world of the supernatural is an essential ingredient of their life, a metaphysical necessity. Out of this land of mists and marshes, forbidding sea and rugged hills, have come tales of dragons and demons, drowned cities and seductresses, giants and human sacrifice, fairies and men of faith. Incongruously, sacred and profane beliefs have actually nurtured one another down the ages, often to the dismay of Church authorities. If there are no saints without legends, it is also true to say that there are few legends without saints.

Little and large

Congenial, sometimes naïve, and often good Christians, giants such as Hok-Bras and Gargantua erected megaliths and even created 'mountains' such as the Monts d'Arrée. Ogres and elves lurk in suspended animation in the remnants of once mighty forests such as Paimpont.

One charming legend tells how fairies, expelled from the Forest of

Brocéliande, shed so many tears that the Golfe du Morbihan was formed. They threw into it their crowns of flowers, which changed into 365 islands, and three of them – Houat, Hoëdic and Belle-Île, the loveliest of the three – drifted out to sea.

Breton fairies are helped by shy little beings called *korrigans*. There are sirens too, eternal temptresses as immortalised in Homer's *Odyssey*.

Heroes

The most famous of heroes is undoubtedly King Arthur, the central character of a romantic cycle of legends in which religion and magic are in perfect harmony and Christian morality is upheld by all – including Merlin the magician. Arthur and his gallant friends were adopted into Breton folklore thanks to Celtic immigrants from Britain, and Arthurian legends are considered by the Bretons to have been based here rather than in Britain.

Sainted men and women

Local saints are considered family friends, and credited with healing powers against all kinds of diseases. Even animals have their own saint to protect them: thus, St Cornély is the patron saint of cattle.

Of the region's important saints, first of all there is St Anne, mother of Mary and patron saint of Brittany. According to legend, she was born in Brittany, went to Judea, married Joachim, gave birth to Mary, and later returned to her native country.

Jesus is said to have brought St Peter here to meet his grandmother.

St Yves is another native, the most popular saint in Brittany. He is patron saint of lawyers and protector of the poor, a combination of interests that confounds modern cynicism.

Culture

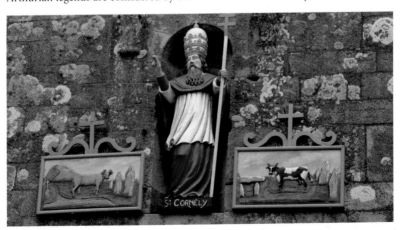

Church of Saint Cornély, the patron saint of livestock, Carnac

Festivals

The names of festivals remind us that most of them are rooted in the basic realities that used to characterise daily life in the past, celebrated because they were the very things that provided people with their livelihood: horses, cider, buckwheat and, above all, the sea, a theme that recurs again and again. These festivals overflow with music and dance, competitions, Celtic games and a selection of gastronomic delights.

Festoù-noz (night parties) are less sophisticated than folk festivals. Once they used to celebrate the completion of rural tasks such as

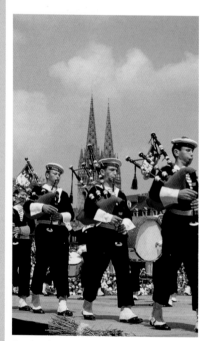

Bagpipes betray the Celtic origins of this festival

the harvest. Today, they still exist as occasions for people to drink and be merry, and especially to dance. The most important festivals take place in Quimper, Lorient and Plozévet.

Festival de Cornouaille takes place in Quimper during the third week of July at the heart of the old town; and 4,000 participants, in various shows, offer music, singing, dancing, fairy tales, Breton games and exhibitions. *Tel: 02 98 55 53 53; www.festival-cornouaille.com*

Festival Interceltique is the major event of southern Brittany, in Lorient during August, with a gathering of more than 4,500 artists from various Celtic countries. All the arts are represented; 10 days of performances take place on stage and also in the streets. *Tel: 02 97 21 24 29; www.festival-interceltique.com*

Mondial'Folk de Plozévet in the small town of Plozévet in Finistère in August draws some 800 dancers, singers and musicians from

14 countries, including the best Breton groups. *Tel: 02 98 91 45 45; www.mondialfolk.org*

Other summer folk festivals and traditional feasts include:

July
Auray: Festival International d'Auray (international folk music), with stage and street performances. *Tel: 02 97 24 09 75.*

Fouesnant: Fête des Pommiers (Apple Tree Festival). *Tel: 02 98 56 00 93.*

Fougères: Voix des pays (a variety of performances). *Tel: 02 99 94 83 65.*

Gourin: Grande Fête de la Crêpe (Pancake Festival). *Tel: 02 97 23 66 33.*

Pont-l'Abbé: Fête des Brodeuses (Embroiderers' Festival). *Tel: 02 98 82 37 99.*

August
Le Croisic: Fête de la Mer (Sea Festival). *Tel: 02 40 23 00 70.*

Douarnenez: Festival International de Folklore (Folk Festival). *Tel: 02 98 92 13 35.*

Guerlesquin: Marché Animé, street performances, every Monday. *Tel: 02 98 72 84 20.*

Guingamp: Fête de la St-Loup: dancing, singing, Breton games and *festoù-noz. Tel: 02 96 43 73 89.*

Lamballe: Festival Folklorique des Ajoncs d'Or (Folk Festival). *Tel: 02 96 31 05 38.*

Roscoff: Fête de la Mer (Sea Festival). *Tel: 02 98 61 12 13.*

St-Briac: Fête des Mouettes (Seagull Festival). *Tel: 02 99 88 07 67.*

Vannes: Fêtes d'Arvor (traditional music and dancing). *Tel: 02 97 42 71 29.*

Festivals

Traditional dance in Pont-l'Abbé

Impressions

The sea is Brittany's greatest attraction: its changing moods are legendary, the views breathtaking, and the air invigorating, while the dense forests, wild moors and solitary mountains are shrouded in mystery, and the clear rivers abound in fish.

In Brittany you can have a holiday that is tailor-made for you: you can be active or relax totally, join the holiday crowds or be completely on your own. You can stay in a lively seaside resort and come back with your hair full of sand, or you can spend a week roaming the countryside in a horse-drawn caravan.

You can enjoy the sophisticated life of Dinard or La Baule, book a room in a castle or stay on a farm. You can cut yourself off from civilisation on one of the fascinating islands, join a keep-fit course in a *thalassothérapie* centre, explore on horseback Brittany's most secluded areas or gallop along the cliff tops and on the beaches at low tide . . . the choice is yours.

When to go

The best time to visit Brittany is in late spring and summer, when the sun shines generously but a sea breeze keeps temperatures around 20°C (68°F). However, the weather can suddenly turn cool and showery. So come prepared and don't forget to bring a cardigan, a raincoat and a pair of comfortable walking shoes, as well as beach clothes and sandals; you will probably use them all in the space of a single day!

Arriving

If you've arrived directly from abroad, don't forget that Brittany is part of France; the pavement cafés, the shops, the food stalls and a quick glance at a restaurant menu will clear any doubt in your mind straight away. Whatever you have heard about the Bretons' spirit of independence, though, remember that they are often as proud of being French as they are of being Bretons!

Lifestyle

Meal times are fairly rigid and restaurants may not serve you if you arrive too late; lunch is generally served from noon to 1.30pm and dinner from 7pm to 10pm.

As everywhere in France, meals are meant to be enjoyed, not rushed through, and you will find that many places, including sights, castles, museums and shops, are usually closed between noon and 2pm, making a definite lull in the day's activities which you will soon learn to appreciate and savour. To compensate for this interruption, shops usually extend their opening hours in the evening during the holiday season, but banks and museums do not.

The end of the season comes rather abruptly during the second half of September, and by the end of the month many sights are closed until the next spring, or sometimes only open at weekends.

Dress is informal except in certain hotels and casinos. Avoid beach clothes inside churches, which are crowded on Sunday mornings and should not be visited then for sightseeing.

People greet each other by shaking hands. They will appreciate your trying to speak French and will then come to your rescue in English if they can.

Local tourist offices will help with information and useful tips.

Prettily patterned half-timbered façades above shops in Brittany's capital, Rennes

Opening times

It is impossible to generalise about church opening times; in theory, churches are open during daytime, but in practice, they are often closed for fear of damage. Sometimes a notice on the door indicates where the key can be obtained, but this is not always the case and you must be prepared for some frustrating experiences when visiting churches.

For information, contact the local tourist offices.

Getting around

Maps

It is important to have a fairly detailed regional map that shows secondary roads and small villages, since prehistoric sites, castles, chapels, churches and open-air museums are often well hidden in the countryside. The best maps are published by Michelin and the Institut Géographique National; both are reasonably priced and available at bookshops, hypermarkets and through newsagents.

The more comprehensive Michelin map number 230 (1/200,000) is useful for visitors with cars, as the clearly graded roads make route-planning easier. The IGN map number 105 (1/250,000) is less detailed, but gives a better overall view of the region, and includes seven town plans.

Driving

Brittany is ideal touring country. Provided you keep away from the main seaside resorts, you'll find lots of quiet roads winding through the countryside. Excursions can be based on various themes. Some of them, such as 'In the painters' footsteps' (*see pp112–13*) or 'Castles of southern Brittany' (*see pp138–9*), are dealt with in this guide, but there are many other possibilities that can be explained by local tourist offices.

Town centres are crowded, and their narrow streets often unsuitable for traffic. To avoid unnecessary delays, leave your car in one of the official car parks (remember to pay for your time at a nearby machine, and display the ticket on your dashboard).

Cycling

Cycling in Brittany can be very enjoyable along the coast and inland except in mountainous areas. Cycle and mountain-bike trips, including accommodation for two to seven nights, are organised by Loisirs Accueil (*see below*).

Walking

Walking in Brittany is particularly rewarding and gives an exhilarating feeling of freedom (*see pp166–7*). There is a wide choice of guided and self-guided hiking tours, organised by Loisirs Accueil, from a weekend along the Côte de Granit Rose to a two-week hike across Brittany from the Golfe du Morbihan on the south coast to Lannion on the north coast.

Comité Départementale du Tourisme des Côtes d'Armor. Tel: 02 96 62 72 15; fax: 02 96 33 59 10; www.cotesdarmor.com

Sailing and cruising

Sailing trips are available all along the coast for beginners and experienced sailors alike, and are a good way to discover Brittany's coastline (information available from tourist offices). Guided cruises from Dinard explore the River Rance on board *Le Chateaubriand* (*tel: 02 99 46 44 40; www.chateaubriand.com*).

Cruise ships frequently visit ports in Brittany as they reposition between the Mediterranean and Baltic in the spring and autumn. For a hands-on sailing experience along the Breton coast, Les Glénans offers week-long courses in French or English (*tel: 01 53 92 86 00; www.glenans.asso.fr*).

Where to go

The Breton Peninsula can be divided into four main areas. To the east are Rennes and the so-called border areas, which used to mark the frontier between France and Brittany and which have a wealth of magnificent defensive castles. It is an area of rolling hills, beautiful woodland and wandering rivers, with the regional capital, Rennes, in its centre.

Facing the coast of Cornwall across the English Channel, northern Brittany has long forgotten the days of privateering and long-distance fishing. Today, the varied coastline, in turn rugged and tame, is lined with fashionable resorts and the historic town of St-Malo. The sunny coast of southern Brittany is edged with long

Walking along the cliff path of Cap Sizun to the Enfer de Plogoff

golden beaches and a vast natural reserve, the Golfe du Morbihan. The countryside is mellow, with river valleys and peaceful old towns. Situated at the head of the busy Loire estuary, Nantes is the region's largest conurbation.

Surrounded by the sea on three sides, Finistère is the most authentically Breton of the four areas, with typical

Bréhat on the northern coast

coastal activities, a firmly established agricultural economy and a culture deeply attached to its traditions.

Seaside resorts have great charm, while the Monts d'Arrée and Montagnes Noires are extremely rich scenically and culturally. At the heart of Cornouaille, Quimper is one of the most attractive towns in Brittany.

Where to find . . .

Far from being exhaustive, the list given below is only a thematically arranged selection of the best sites, monuments, etc.

Abbeys: Landévennec (Crozon Peninsula), St-Gildas-de-Rhuys.

Beaches: Dinard, St-Lunaire, St-Cast-le-Guildo, Le Val-André, Trégastel-Plage (north coast); Bénodet, Mousterlin, Beg Meil, Cap Coz (south Finistère); Quiberon, La Trinité-sur-Mer, La Baule (south coast).

Bird sanctuaries: Les Sept Îles (off the Côte de Granit Rose), Golfe du Morbihan (south coast).

Calvaries: Plougastel-Daoulas and Tronoën (Finistère), Guéhenno (Morbihan, north of Vannes).

Castles: Combourg, Montmuran (north of Rennes), Les Rochers-Sévigné (east of Rennes), Fougères, Vitré, Fort la Latte (west of Dinard), La Roche-Jagu (near Tréguier), Kerjean (south of Roscoff), Josselin (near Ploërmel), Suscinio (Rhuys Peninsula), Nantes.

Churches: Quimper, Tréguier and Dol cathedrals, St-Sauveur (Dinan), Kreisker Chapel (St-Pol-de-Léon), Runan (north of Guingamp), St-Herbot (south of Morlaix), Pont-Croix (southwest of Douarnenez), Loctudy (south Finistère), Ste-Barbe (north of Quimperlé), Ste-Noyale (northeast of Pontivy).

Church interiors: Lamballe, Loc-Envel (west of Guingamp), Notre-Dame-du-Tertre (Châtelaudren, *see p147*), Kerfons (south of Lannion), Lampaul-Guimiliau (south of Morlaix), St-Fiacre, Kernascléden (north of Quimperlé).

Cliffs: Cap Fréhel (north coast), Crozon Peninsula, Pointe du Raz (Finistère).

Domestic architecture: Granite – Locronan (north of Quimper), Rochefort-en-Terre (east of Vannes). Timber-framed – Quimper, Morlaix, Rennes, Dol-de-Bretagne.

Fishing rivers: Léguer and Trieux (north coast, salmon and trout), Aulne (Finistère, salmon), Scorff (trout), Blavet (south coast, salmon).

Forests: Paimpont (west of Rennes), Huelgoat (Finistère), Quénécan (Lac de Guerlédan).

Islands: Bréhat (north coast), Ouessant and Sein (Finistère), Belle-Île (south coast).

Lakes: Guerlédan (north of Pontivy).

Megaliths: La Roche-aux-Fées (south of Rennes), Barnenez (north of Morlaix), Lagatjar (Crozon Peninsula), Carnac and Locmariaquer (south coast).

Oyster beds: Cancale (north coast), Etel and Pénerf rivers (south coast).

Parish closes: St-Thégonnec, Guimiliau, Pleyben (Finistère).

Parks and gardens: Caradeuc (north-west of Rennes), Les Rochers-Sévigné, Kerguéhennec (west of Ploërmel).

Walled cities: St-Malo, Dinan, Concarneau, Vannes, Guérande.

A shopping street in Vannes

Rennes and the east

The eastern part of Brittany, which has Rennes as its main town, is the region least influenced by the sea, but is Breton all the same. The limits of this 'border area' adjoining the rest of France are roughly those of the Ille-et-Vilaine département (its small section of coastline, which belongs to the Côte d'Emeraude, is dealt with under northern Brittany).

Rural image

Named after the two main rivers that flow through it and meet in Rennes, Ille-et-Vilaine is in many ways a transition area. Its rolling hills and rich pastures are not unlike those of Normandy, its close neighbour to the northeast, while its lazy winding rivers are reminiscent of the Loire region to the south.

However, the woodland areas are unmistakably Breton, and still evoke the mystery of Celtic legends. The Paimpont Forest of today is but a remnant of the dense Brocéliande, one of ancient Europe's finest hunting forests which once cloaked most of inland Brittany. Where else but here could you expect to see the fountain where Merlin the Magician first met the beautiful Viviane?

Difficult dual role

The Rennes region still bears evidence of the double role it played throughout its troubled history as the gateway to Brittany and the first line of defence against intruders from the east. All the ambiguity of this dual function is contained in the expression used by the well-loved Duchess Anne, who, when referring to the mighty fortress of Fougères, called it 'the key to my treasure'. But did she intend to use that key to lock up her treasure or, on the contrary, to unlock the door and let visitors in? Much later the area was again at the heart of political strife when, during the French Revolution, there was fierce fighting between French troops and Breton royalists trying to keep them out of Brittany.

Cultural melting pot

By virtue of its location, the region has always been more open to outside influences than the rest of Brittany. As early as the Middle Ages, pilgrims on their way to Santiago de Compostela in Spain went right through it, traditionally stopping at Dol-de-Bretagne in the north and Redon in the south.

The French language was adopted more readily in Ille-et-Vilaine than in Basse (Lower) Bretagne, and today few people speak Breton here.

Moreover, every year, when Rennes and its region stage splendid festivals, some of the best and most colourful Breton traditions are displayed side by side with those from other regions of Brittany. Considerable economic development and improved communications in Rennes in the last 30 years have enhanced the region's role as the gateway to Brittany.

Rennes and the east

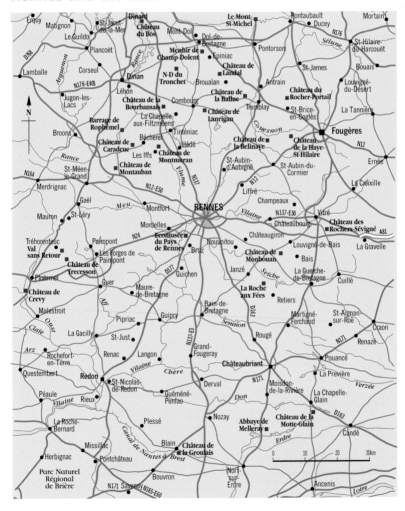

RENNES

Rennes was founded by the Celts 2,000 years ago at the centre of a rich agricultural basin where the Ille and Vilaine rivers meet. When Brittany became a duchy, both Rennes and Nantes claimed the title of capital, and the struggle for supremacy went on for centuries.

After the signing of the Treaty of Union between France and Brittany in 1532, the city became the seat of the Breton parliament and the region's cultural and administrative centre. Marking its new status, elegant stone buildings were erected next to the timber-framed houses. But the centre was destroyed by fire in 1720 and rebuilt shortly afterwards in French classical style with broad open spaces.

During the 19th century, the town spread south of the Vilaine and the university was founded. The designation of Rennes as the capital of Brittany in 1956 put an end to centuries of rivalry with Nantes. It also marked the beginning of the city's economic revival. Improved communications gave Rennes a chance to invest in high technology and develop traditional industries such as the car industry (Citroën), the food industry and publishing (*Ouest-France* is France's biggest-selling daily newspaper).

Rennes' population has already exceeded the 270,000 mark and the town is still expanding, while preserving its historic centre situated on the right bank of the Vilaine. This can be divided into two distinct parts: old Rennes and the adjoining 18th-century town.

The austere façade of the Palais de Justice

Rennes

Old Rennes

This is essentially located round the cathedral. The Portes Mordelaises nearby is all that remains of the town walls.

Cathédrale St-Pierre

The two towers are the only remaining parts of the original building dating from the 16th and 17th centuries, since the cathedral was rebuilt at the end of the 18th century and the interior richly decorated. Note the 16th-century Flemish altarpiece.

Carrefour de la Cathédrale.
Open: daily 9.30am–noon & 3–6pm.

Medieval streets

Behind the cathedral, several narrow streets have medieval and Renaissance half-timbered houses, some of them corbelled, with beautifully carved beams. The most picturesque streets are the rue St-Yves, rue du Chapitre, rue de

Rennes is situated 347km (216 miles) southwest of Paris via the A11 and A81 motorways and 71km (44 miles) south of the Channel port of St-Malo, which has regular ferry crossings from Portsmouth, Poole, Jersey and Guernsey. It is two hours from Paris by TGV (fast train). There are direct flights to Rennes/St-Jacques Airport from Paris, London and most large French towns.

The Thabor Gardens, a pleasure in any season

carved wood panelling, coffered ceilings and paintings. The Grande-Chambre is the most remarkable hall in the palace. When the architect Gabriel rebuilt Rennes in the 18th century, he slightly altered the façade. In 1994 the palace was devastated by a fire, but has now been restored to its full glory.
Place du Palais. Worthwhile afternoon guided tours must be arranged through the Office de Tourisme. Tel: 02 99 67 11 66. Admission charge.

The 18th-century town

The architect of the 'new' town was Gabriel, who designed the place de la Concorde in Paris. Its centre is the vast place de la Mairie, featuring the town hall and the theatre.

Église Notre-Dame-en-St-Melaine and Jardin du Thabor

St-Melaine, to the east of the town centre, is a former abbey church. The tower and the intersection between the nave and the transept date from the 11th century. Inside, a 15th-century fresco depicts Christ's baptism. On the north side are the 17th-century cloisters.

The Thabor Gardens, in the abbey grounds, were a favourite haunt of Romantic writer Chateaubriand (*see p50*). Its 3,122 named species are in a formal French garden, a rose garden and an English-style park.
Place St-Melaine.
Church: tel: 02 99 67 11 11.
Open: daily 8.30am–7pm.

la Psalette and rue St-Guillaume, where you can admire the remarkable 16th-century house known as Du Guesclin's House. At the end of the rue du Chapitre, on the edge of the medieval quarter, the imposing 18th-century Hôtel de Blossac offers a marked contrast with the neighbouring houses.

North of the cathedral, the long place des Lices, which was used for tournaments in medieval times, is surrounded by several 17th-century residences built for members of the Breton parliament. The old town extends further north along the rue St-Michel to the place Ste-Anne.

Palais de Justice

This magnificent edifice marks the transition between the old town and the 18th-century town. It was built between 1618 and 1655 by Salomon de Brosse, the architect of the Luxembourg Palace in Paris, to house the Breton parliament. Austere outside, it is lavishly decorated inside with gilt

Gardens open: daily 7.30am–6pm, until 8pm in summer. Free admission.

Hôtel de Ville (Town hall)

The town hall was built in Louis XV style between 1734 and 1743. At the centre of the elegant curved façade stands an imposing belfry; below the pediment, an empty recess originally contained a bronze statue of Louis XV, destroyed during the Revolution. In the left wing, 18th-century tapestries from Brussels hang over the staircase, and the Great Hall is decorated with symbols of Breton cities. Facing the town hall across the square, the theatre (open for performances) was built in 1832.
Place de la Mairie. Tel: 02 99 67 11 11. Open: Mon–Fri 9am–5pm. Closed: Sat & Sun. Admission charge.

Musée des Beaux-Arts and Musée de Bretagne

Both are situated on the south bank of the river, in a former university

The grand town hall, in the classical quarter

building dating from the 19th century. The Musée des Beaux-Arts contains an important collection of paintings from the 14th to the 20th centuries, with masterpieces such as *Perseus and Andromeda* by Veronese, *Tête de Femme* by Picasso, and works by Corot, Boudin, Sisley, Gauguin and the School of Pont-Aven. The jewel of the collection is the *Nouveau-Né* by the 17th-century French painter Georges de la Tour, a moving study of two women watching over a new-born baby.

The Musée de Bretagne is a regional museum illustrating Brittany's history through various objects, documents, sculptures, jewellery and handicrafts. There are six sections: Prehistory, Gallo-Roman Armorique, the Middle Ages, the Ancien Régime (1532–1789), the 19th Century, and Brittany Today.
Musée des Beaux-Arts, 20 quai Émile-Zola. Tel: 02 23 62 17 45; www.mbar.org. Open: 10am–noon & 2–6pm. Closed: Mon & holidays. Admission charge. Musée de Bretagne. Tel: 02 23 40 66 70; www.musee-bretagne.fr. Open: Tue noon–9pm, Wed–Fri noon–7pm, Sat & Sun 2–7pm. Closed: Mon. Admission charge.

Nearby
Ecomusée du Pays de Rennes

This open-air museum, 8km (5 miles) south of Rennes, illustrates the history of farming from the 16th century on.
Route de Châtillon-sur-Seiche, 35200 Rennes. Tel: 02 99 51 38 15;

(cont on p34)

Castles and manor houses

Josselin on the Oust

Touring Brittany, you can spot a castle round almost every bend of the road. Some hide behind a screen of foliage, others open their gates to offer a close-up view of their exterior. A few can be visited, and it is a thrilling experience to wander through bare, chill rooms or tastefully furnished halls and libraries full of leather-bound volumes. For these dwellings of bygone days hold within their walls evidence of the lives of their often forgotten occupants.

Some 4,000 castles in Brittany reflect the changing lifestyle and the economic ups and downs of a society through ten centuries of war and peace. Changes in architectural styles were prompted not only by necessity but also by fashion, for in spite of Brittany's prolonged isolation, main artistic trends flourishing in France and Italy influenced master builders and landowners, who brought back new ideas from their extensive travels. Thus, Madame de Sévigné introduced the comfort and elegance of the French court in her beloved castle of Les Rochers-Sévigné near Vitré.

Whatever their style, Brittany's castles all bear an undeniable stamp of authenticity: the granite with which they were built – often with contrasting white sandstone.

Defensive fortresses

Defensive fortresses were erected by feudal lords in strategic places – on a river bank, like Josselin in Morbihan, or on a promontory facing the sea, like Fort la Latte near Cap Fréhel. Some castles were built by the dukes of Brittany or came into their possession, and a fortified town grew up around them, as in Dinan and Fougères.

Splendid residences

Once the threat of war had abated, castles became a symbol of prosperity and of political power. Many, like Caradeuc near Bécherel and La Bourbansais south of Dinan, were built by influential members of the Breton parliament during the 17th and 18th centuries. At the end of the 19th century, an exaggerated taste for grandeur led to the building of such follies as Trévarez at the heart of the Montagnes Noires.

At the same time a great variety of more modest edifices mushroomed all over the countryside. These manor houses were the homes of the less affluent Breton nobility or the country houses of rich shipowners, usually based in St-Malo. Two of the best examples are the Château du Bos, south of St-Malo, and the Manoir de Kérazan, near Loctudy in south Finistère.

For information on castles visit: *www.casteland.com/pfr/chateau/ bretagne*

Vitré on the Vilaine

www.ecomusee-rennes-metropole.fr. Open: Apr–Sept daily 9am–6pm; Oct–Mar Tue–Fri 9am–noon & 2–6pm, Sat & Sun 2–6pm. Closed: Mon. Admission charge.

Parc Ornithologique de Bretagne

Located at Bruz, 12km (7 miles) south of Rennes, the park has a fascinating collection of exotic birds.

53 boulevard Pasteur, 35170 Bruz. Tel: 02 99 52 68 57; www.parc-ornithologique.com. Open: July & Aug daily 10am–noon & 2–7pm; Apr–June & Sept 2–7pm. Admission charge.

Ancenis

Ancenis was the site of an important castle in the first line of defence of the Duchy of Brittany in the Loire region. Building began in 982. Then, during the 12th century, having married his son Geoffrey to the young Duchess of Brittany, Henry II of England ruled over Brittany and extended the castle to strengthen his defences. Partly dismantled by Anne of Brittany in 1490, Ancenis was rebuilt at the end of the 16th century. You can still see the fortified walls, the two machicolated gate towers, the covered drawbridge and the Grand Logis (residential building) in Renaissance style.

142km (88 miles) southeast of Rennes.

Antrain

Antrain dominates the rivers Couesnon and Loisance from its strategic location on high ground. The village church, built in the 12th century, was fortified in the 15th century to help in the defence of the duchy. The Romanesque front portal is remarkable, with rounded archivolt (ornamental moulding round an arch) and side columns with carved capitals. The domed steeple was added in the 17th century. The decoration of the chancel dates from the 18th century.

Château de Bonne-Fontaine, a 16th-century feudal manor house just south of Antrain

The impressive ruins of La Groulais Castle – still standing despite all Richelieu's efforts to raze it

Blain

Blain lies on the north bank of the Nantes–Brest Canal, between Nantes and Redon. The town's commercial tradition goes back to the Roman occupation.

Château de la Groulais

Situated on the south bank of the canal, the castle was built in the 12th century as part of the second line of defence along the border between France and Brittany. Remodelled in the 14th and 15th centuries, the castle belonged to the powerful Rohan family and was partly dismantled in 1628 by Richelieu, whose policy was to eliminate any threat to the king's power.

The ruins include several towers and part of the walls, the 14th-century keep and the Logis du Roi, with its typically Renaissance high dormer windows and tall red-brick chimneys.
Tel: 02 40 79 07 81. Open: Apr–Oct 10am–noon & 2.30–6.30pm. Closed: Mon. Admission charge.

Musée des Arts et Traditions Populaires du Pays Blinois

This museum illustrates local history from the Gallo-Roman period with archaeological finds, everyday objects and a reconstruction of the town's main square surrounded by traditional shops.
2 place J Guihard. Tel: 02 40 79 98 51. Open: 2–6pm. Closed: Sun & Mon. Admission charge.

Blain is 81km (50 miles) south of Rennes on the D164 to Redon.

Château de la Ballue

Dating from the 17th century, this castle was one of the headquarters of the royalist Chouans during the Revolution. Now an elegant hotel, the gardens are open to the public.
5km (3 miles) southwest of Antrain. Tel: 02 99 97 47 86; www.laballuegarden.com. Open: mid-Mar–Nov daily 10.30am–6.30pm, tours. Admission charge.

Tremblay

In the village is another Romanesque church, remodelled in the 16th century. Note the large cross over the main altar.
4km (2¹/₂ miles) south of Antrain on the D175.

Antrain is 45km (28 miles) northeast of Rennes on the D175.

Bécherel

See p147.

Château de la Bourbansais

Built during the 17th and 18th centuries, this impressive residential castle is flanked by two low, round towers and surmounted by the pointed roof of the stair tower. The castle is famous for its French-style gardens and its large open-air zoo.

Like the outside, the interior illustrates the wealth and ambition of the Breton parliament members who built it: exquisite 18th-century furniture, 17th-century Aubusson tapestries and fine china.

Pleugueneuc, 16km (10 miles) southeast of Dinan on the N137. Tel: 02 99 69 40 07; www.labourbansais.com. Open: Apr–Sept daily, five guided tours from 11.15am. Zoo open: Apr–Sept daily 10am–7pm. Call or check website for timings during other months. Admission charge.

Châteaubriant

Once a major border stronghold, the town developed around its powerful castle, on the banks of the River Chère, and still lives in its shadow.

Château

The castle is in two parts, separated by a formal garden. The medieval fortress, built in the 11th century and surrounded by a fortified wall, includes a massive square keep flanked by the 15th-century Grand Logis and a 13th-century chapel and gatehouse.

The Renaissance buildings were inspired by the beautiful castles of the Loire. They were built by Jean de Laval, Count of Châteaubriant and Governor of Brittany, who is mainly remembered for the gruesome role he played in a tragic story involving his wife, Françoise de Foix. Jealously guarded by a husband she had married at the age of 11, she was lured to the French court and became the mistress of François I. When the king tired of her, she returned to Châteaubriant, who cruelly kept her imprisoned until she died ten years later.

Rue du Château. Tel: 02 40 28 20 20. Open: May–Sept 11am–6.30pm; Oct–Apr 2–5pm, guided tours. Closed: Tue. Admission charge. Grounds open: 8am–6pm daily (later in summer). Free admission.

Église St-Jean de Béré

Situated on the other side of the river, this Romanesque church contains several fine 15th- and 17th-century statues and some elaborate altarpieces from the late 17th century.

The remains of the castle at Châteaugiron, often besieged down the centuries

Châteaubriant is 65km (40 miles) north of Nantes on the D178.

Châteaugiron

The town and its mighty castle were ransacked during the Wars of Religion at the end of the 16th century. However, in the 17th century, the manufacture of canvas brought new prosperity to the town. You can still see some of the half-timbered houses of the merchants, principally along the main street.

Château

The impressive 38m (125ft) high round keep, dating from the 13th century, stands apart from the other remaining medieval buildings: the 12th-century chapel, the clock tower and two other 15th-century machicolated towers. The residential building, erected in the 18th century, is now the town hall, which also houses the tourist information office.
Tel: 02 99 37 89 02; www.ville-chateaugiron.fr. Open: July & Aug daily, tours at 10.30am, 2.30pm & 4.30pm, or ask at tourist office. Sun at 3.30pm in June. Admission charge.

Châteaugiron is 15km (9 miles) southeast of Rennes on the D463.

Combourg

The romantic figure of Chateaubriand (*see p50*) is linked to the town of Combourg, which nestles on the edge of a peaceful lake below an imposing medieval castle. You will get the best overall view from across the lake. With a little imagination, you could recapture the intense, solitary mood that prompted the young Chateaubriand to say later in his famous *Mémoires d'Outre-Tombe*: 'It was in the woods of Combourg that I became what I am today.'

Château

Chateaubriand lived for two years – in almost complete isolation, with his parents and his sister Lucile, his sole companion – in the awe-inspiring fortress. It is no wonder the adolescent Chateaubriand was stirred by it.

Built in the 11th century by the Bishop of Dol, and extended and remodelled in the 14th and 15th centuries, Combourg Castle was bought by Chateaubriand's father; his descendants still live there.

The austere feudal appearance of the castle is marked by four massive towers linked by high crenellated walls. Inside, visitors can see various mementoes of the poet in the Salle des Archives and climb up the 'haunted' Tour du Chat to the bedroom where he listened to the howl of the wind.
*Rue des Princes. Tel: 02 99 73 22 95; www.combourg.net.
Château open: Apr–Oct 2–5.30pm, guided tours. Closed: Sat except July & Aug. Admission charge.
Park open: Apr–Oct 9–noon & 2–6pm. Closed: Sat except July & Aug. Free admission.*

The slopes of modest Mont-Dol have yielded prehistoric animal remains and human tools

Combourg is 17km (11 miles) south of Dol-de-Bretagne on the D795. www.combourg.net

Dinan

See pp46–7.

Dol-de-Bretagne

This small provincial town was an important religious centre during the Middle Ages, and the starting point of the Tro Breiz (Tour of Brittany), a pilgrimage round Brittany's cathedrals which a Breton felt compelled to make at least once in his life.

Today, pilgrims have been replaced by tourists who come to admire the medieval streets (Grande Rue des Stuarts and rue Ceinte), lined with half-timbered houses and the wonderful Gothic cathedral.

Cathédrale St-Samson

Erected in the 13th and 14th centuries, the early Gothic edifice shows a strong Norman influence. On the south side a small 13th-century porch offers an interesting contrast with the remarkable 14th-century porch surmounted by a Flamboyant balustrade.

The lofty 100m (328ft) long nave is impressive, and the chancel is enhanced by beautiful 14th-century stained-glass panels.
Place de la Cathédrale.

CathédralOscope

Halfway between St-Malo and Le Mont-St-Michel is the only cultural centre in Europe devoted to the architecture, construction and symbolism of cathedrals. The viewing platform on the second floor affords wonderful views of the cathedral of Dol-de-Bretagne.
Place de la Cathédrale, 35120 Dol-de-Bretagne. Tel: 02 99 48 35 30.
Open: Apr–Oct daily 10am–12.30pm & 1.30–7pm. Admission charge.

Menhir de Champ-Dolent

This free-standing stone, set in the 'Field of Grief', is one of the finest megaliths in Brittany. It stands alone in a field, evidence of early man.
1.5km (1 mile) south on the D795.

Mont-Dol

This steep granite mound, 65m (213ft) high, offers a panoramic view of the whole of Mont-St-Michel Bay.
2km (1¼ miles) north of Dol on the D155.

Dol-de-Bretagne is 25km (16 miles) southeast of St-Malo on the D4.

Forêt du Gâvre

See p141.

Fougères

Once, Fougères was the main border fortress defending the Duchy of Brittany and a prosperous market town. Later, it became an important centre for the manufacture of canvas. Then, following a slowdown in the canvas industry, Fougères moved successfully into the shoe industry.

Today, wise investments in high-tech industries have enabled the city to flourish once again and restore its architectural heritage.

Château

Built in the 12th century, the castle – one of the largest in Europe – stands on a rocky peninsula within a deep bend of the River Nançon. Extended in the 13th, 14th and 15th centuries, its impressive fortifications, including 13 towers, are remarkable examples of medieval military architecture.

The low but wide south towers facing St-Sulpice church were intended to house heavy guns, and contrast with the 31m (102ft) high Tour Melusine built a century earlier.

Past the main gate, a second line of defence barred the entrance to the main courtyard where the residential quarters stood, next to the chapel and the well. The last line of defence protected the keep and the emergency exit.
Place Pierre Symon. Tel: 02 99 99 79 59; www.ot-fougeres.fr. Open: daily mid-June–mid-Sept 9am–7pm; mid-Sept–Dec & Feb–mid-June 10am–noon & 2–5pm, guided tours. Closed: Jan. Admission charge.

Haute Ville

Situated across the river, the 'high town' dominates the castle and the medieval quarter. At one end of the rue Nationale stands the **Église St-Léonard**, dating from the 16th century, surmounted by a 17th-century tower. Next to it is the 16th-century town hall. At right angles to the rue Nationale, the rue de la Pinterie leading down to the castle has some 18th-century residences.

The **Musée de la Villéon** is devoted to the Impressionist painter Emmanuel de la Villéon (1858–1954), a native of Fougères.

Fougères, an old shoe-making town, found favour with the writers Balzac and Victor Hugo

Rue Nationale. Tel: 02 99 99 19 98.
Open: mid-June–mid-Sept daily
10am–12.30pm & 2–6pm; mid-Sept–
mid-June Wed–Sun 10am–noon &
2–5pm. Closed: Mon & Tue.
Free admission.

Behind the covered market, in the rue
Nationale, the Belfry is an interesting
octagonal tower dating from the 14th
and 15th centuries. However, it is not
open to the public.

Medieval town

The medieval town lies south of the
castle. The **Église St-Sulpice**, built in
Flamboyant Gothic style, contains
two splendid granite retables and a
charming statue of the Virgin Mary
feeding her Child. The place du
Marchix has been the town's market
square since medieval times. The
surrounding streets are lined with 16th-
century half-timbered houses.

Mellé

A designated Rural Patrimony
Commune, Mellé has organised

Hédé's church is Romanesque and contains a
17th-century alabaster statue of the Virgin

walking tours of its immaculate stone
village and surrounding countryside
as well the **Maison Pierres et Nature**
museum, geared towards younger
visitors, explaining various aspects of
regional rural life.
Tel: 02 99 17 14 24. Open: June–Sept
daily 2–6pm; Apr & May weekends &
holidays 2–6pm. Admission charge.

Fougères is 48km (30 miles) northeast of
Rennes on the N12.

Grand-Fougeray

Of its once-powerful castle, there
remains one of the most remarkable
medieval keeps in Brittany. Built in the
14th century, the tall, round structure
has a protruding stair turret linking the
four vaulted storeys. It is known as the
Tour du Guesclin because it was seized
by surprise from the English by
Bertrand du Guesclin during the
Hundred Years' War. The keep is located
in the midst of a public arboretum.
Tel: 02 99 08 40 19. Open: July & Aug
3–7pm, guided tour. Closed: Mon &
14 July. Visit off-season by appointment.
Admission charge. Arboretum open: all
year round. Free admission.

Chapelle Ste-Agathe

In Langon, 12km (7 miles) west on
the D56, on the village square next
to the Romanesque parish church,
stands the small Chapelle Ste-Agathe.
Because of its fresco dating from the
Gallo-Roman period, it is known as the
Temple of Venus.

The ruins of the medieval castle look out over the town of Hédé

Grand-Fougeray is 42km (26 miles) south of Rennes, just off the N137.

La Guerche-de-Bretagne

Since the 12th century, an important weekly market (Tuesdays) has livened the centre of La Guerche. It has 16th- and 17th-century half-timbered houses and a partly Romanesque church with a set of beautiful 16th-century choir stalls.
32km (20 miles) southeast of Rennes on the D463.

Hédé

Situated between a lake and the canal linking the rivers Ille and Rance, Hédé village clings to a hilltop crowned by a ruined castle. The surrounding area is very attractive, with fine walks. Here you can watch river traffic negotiating a succession of 11 locks with a total difference in level of 27m (89ft). The N795 crosses the canal at La Madeleine, which affords the best view of the locks.

Near Hédé are several picturesque villages, including Bécherel (*see p147*), Les Iffs (*see below*) and Tinténiac in a lovely riverside setting, as well as some fine castles: Combourg (*see p37*), La Bourbansais (*see p36*), Caradeuc (near Bécherel) and Montmuran (*see below*).
20km (12 miles) northwest of Rennes.

Les Iffs

The village of Les Iffs is famous for the richly coloured stained-glass panels that decorate the Gothic church, in particular those of the chancel depicting the Passion, and, in the south transept, the martyrdom of St John the Baptist. Dating from the 16th century, they are the works of local craftsmen who were inspired by Dutch and Italian masters.

Château de Montmuran

This well-preserved castle just north of the village is a pleasing blend of austere medieval military architecture and of more refined 17th- and 18th-century domestic architecture. The machicolated gatehouse and drawbridge (in full working order) are quite impressive. The name of du Guesclin is linked to the castle at several points in history: in 1354 he was knighted in the chapel for his successes against the English; then, as a famous soldier 19 years later, he married the owner, Jeanne de Laval.
Tel: 02 99 45 88 88; www.chateau-montmuran.com. Open: June–Sept 2–6pm. Closed: Sat. Admission charge.

Les Iffs is 8km (5 miles) west of Hédé.

The pleasure-boat harbour of Redon, where landlubbers can envy the pace and style of life afloat

Louvigné-de-Bais

The Gothic church built in the 16th century has superb stained-glass windows, in the finest tradition of Breton craftsmanship, and an altarpiece from the 17th century.

Château de Monbouan

Surrounded by a magnificent park, this charming late 18th-century residence is unpretentious, yet its interior reveals all the grace and elegance of the Louis XV style.

Particularly remarkable within the château are the main stairs, which have been enhanced by a beautiful wrought-iron banister and paintings after Boucher.

Moulins, 5km (3 miles) south by the D777. Tel: 02 99 49 01 56. Open: mid-July–Aug daily 9am–noon & 2–6pm, guided tours. Admission charge.

Louvigné-de-Bais is 12km (7 miles) southwest of Vitré on the D777.

Melleray

Built on the shores of a lovely lake, Melleray is a Cistercian abbey founded in 1142 and considerably remodelled in the 18th century. The austere Cistercian character of the church has been tempered inside by pink granite pillars and white stone vaulting.

22km (14 miles) south of Châteaubriant on the D178 to La Meilleraye-de-Bretagne, then the D18. Church open: for services only, possible visit to the library; try your luck at the gate.

Motte-Glain

Built on the edge of a lake by a member of the powerful Rohan family at the end of the 15th century, the **Château de la Motte-Glain** marks the transition between the feudal castle and the residential manor. The machicolations at the top of the elegant gatehouse serve more as a decoration than defence, and the tall dormer windows and conical roofs of the round towers seem designed to make fun of medieval austerity.

La Chapelle-Glain, 20km (12 miles) southeast of Châteaubriant on the D163, then the D878. Tel: 02 40 55 52 01. Open: mid-June–mid-Sept 2.30–6.30pm, guided tours. Closed: Tue. Admission charge.

Paimpont Forest

See p142.

Redon

A relaxed holiday atmosphere permeates Redon, once a busy

commercial port at the junction of the River Vilaine and the Nantes–Brest Canal and now a restful haven for yachts, cabin cruisers and houseboats. The town has gone into floral decoration in a big way along its cobbled streets and bridges, and has several times won first prize in the national Villes Fleuries competition.

Activity reaches its climax on market day (Monday), when crowds of holidaymakers rub shoulders with the locals among the colourful stands.

Part of the old town is pedestrianised, perfect for admiring the splendid 16th-century half-timbered houses along the Grande Rue and adjacent streets. In the harbour area, the stately three-storey shipowners' houses along quai Duguay-Trouin have lovely wrought-iron balconies and elegant dormer windows. In the rue du Port at the back, you can see the *greniers à sel*, former warehouses used to stock salt from Guérande (*see p127*) on the south coast.

Musée de la Batellerie de l'Ouest

This museum is devoted to the daily life of mariners in the past and includes three barges, two of them afloat.

12 quai Jean-Bart. Tel: 02 99 72 30 95. Open: mid-June–mid-Sept daily 10am–noon & 3–6pm; mid-Sept–mid-June Sat–Mon & Wed 2–6pm. Admission charge.

St-Sauveur

This former abbey church, dating from the 11th century, has a beautiful arcaded Romanesque tower, a blend of strength, simplicity and artistic inspiration. A fire destroyed part of the nave in 1780, isolating the tall Gothic tower. Note the 17th-century retable in the Gothic chancel. The cloister also dates from the early 17th century.

Place St-Sauveur.

Redon is 66km (41 miles) southwest of Rennes on the D177.

La Roche aux Fées

The peaceful wooded setting helps to surround this impressive prehistoric monument with the kind of poetic mystery that sets the Breton imagination working. In this case it would seem that fairies were responsible for putting together some of the enormous blocks of purple schist, the heaviest weighing 40–45 tonnes. The

La Roche aux Fées has a low corridor ending in a tall room; some rocks weigh up to 45 tonnes

fairies went to fetch them in the Forêt du Theil, 5km (3 miles) south, and carried them back in their aprons!
14km (9 miles) west of La Guerche-de-Bretagne.

St-Aubin-du-Cormier

This small city was the scene of the Duke of Brittany's last stand against the French monarchy in 1488. Beaten and humiliated, he died shortly after the battle, leaving his 12-year-old daughter, Anne, in charge. It was only a question of time before Brittany became a French province.

Today, you can still see the ruins of the formidable castle (not open), whose dismantlement was ordered by Charles VIII after the battle. The mutilated keep stands high above the crumbled walls, a symbol of crushed ambitions.
20km (12 miles) southwest of Fougères on the N12 and 23km (14 miles) northwest of Vitré on the D794.

St-Just

Megaliths of all shapes and sizes are scattered over a wide area of heaths

The rue Beaudrairie, Vitré's most fascinating street, is packed with many curious buildings

and pine woods around the village of St-Just. Erected around 4500 BC, the megaliths were in use until the Bronze Age. Long before archaeologists carried out excavations, the Bretons had been inventing poetic legends to satisfy their own curiosity. Thus, Les Demoiselles de Cojoux – a group of three stones, two standing and one on its side – are unfortunate young girls who were turned to stone for having gone dancing on the heath instead of to church.

A network of marked footpaths leads to the Étang du Val, a pretty lake west of St-Just, overlooked by steep rock formations popular with climbing enthusiasts.
8km (5 miles) northeast of Redon on the D177 and D65. Information centre open: July & Aug. Guided tours: Wed & Sun. Admission charge.

Vitré

'Were I not the King of France, I would like to be a citizen of Vitré,' declared Henri IV at the end of the 16th century. Although this popular king was fond of making sweeping statements – being a southerner, he was prone to exaggeration – he was obviously impressed.

The well-defended border town became a thriving commercial centre, exporting canvas all over the world, as well as one of the few Protestant towns in Brittany (which partly explains Henri IV's enthusiasm, since he was a Huguenot). The rich merchants' stone and half-timbered houses still

line narrow streets such as the rue
Beaudrairie and rue d'Embas, close
to the castle.

Champeaux

Built by a noble Breton family who had
a castle nearby, the church is a rare
example of Renaissance art in Brittany,
in particular the stained glass and the
elaborate funeral monument of Guy
d'Espinay and his wife.
*9km (6 miles) northwest of Vitré on
the D29.*

Château

This imposing triangular fortress,
founded in the 11th century but mostly
rebuilt during the 13th and 14th
centuries, was defended by several
towers. The Tour de l'Oratoire houses
a 16th-century triptych decorated with
enamels from Limoges; the Tour St-
Laurent is now a museum that contains
a collection of sculptures which belong
to various houses in town.
*Place du Château. Tel: 02 99 75 04 54;
www.ot-vitre.fr. Open: May–Sept
10am–12.45pm & 2–6pm; Oct–Apr
10am–12.15pm & 2–5.30pm. Closed:
morning Sun & all day Tue.
Admission charge.*

Château des Rochers-Sévigné

This is where Madame de Sévigné
wrote letters to her married daughter.
This witty and often sarcastic account
of provincial life in the 17th century
was later published. The castle contains
mementoes of the writer, who used to

love strolling in her French garden
(designed by Le Nôtre).
*6km (4 miles) southeast of Vitré on the
D88. Tel: 02 99 75 04 54; www.ot-
vitre.fr. Open: May–Sept 10am–12.45pm
& 2–6pm; Oct–Apr 10am–12.15pm &
2–5.30pm. Closed: morning Sun & all
day Tue. Admission charge.*

Église de Notre-Dame

This 15th/16th-century church contains
a remarkable Renaissance stained-glass
window illustrating Christ's arrival
in Jerusalem. The stone pulpit that
decorates the beautiful gabled south
wall was apparently built so that the
clergy could preach directly to the
people and counteract the Protestants'
evil influence!
Place Notre-Dame.

*Vitré is 37km (23 miles) east of Rennes
on the D857.*

Standing since the Stone Age, the megaliths of
St-Just are set off by a blaze of spiny gorse

Walk: Dinan

Still enclosed within its granite walls, Dinan is the best-preserved medieval city in Brittany, and a stroll through the old town is like a journey back in time.

Allow 2 hours.

Start from the place du Guesclin, where you will find parking facilities.

1 Place du Guesclin and Place du Champ

In medieval times, these two adjacent squares formed the city's fairground. In 1357, du Guesclin fought the English knight Thomas of Canterbury in single combat in front of the Duke of Lancaster, who had besieged Dinan. Du Guesclin defeated the knight and thus won the liberation of the city, as well as the admiration of the young Tiphaine, whom he married.
Walk along the rue du Château to the castle on your right.

2 Château

Linked to the town walls, the castle was built in the 14th century.
It is now a museum with splendid views.
Tel: 02 96 39 45 20; www.dinan-tourisme.com. Open: daily June–Sept 10am–6.30pm; Oct–Dec & Feb–May 1.30–5.30pm. Closed: Jan. Return to the rue du Château and continue on rue du Général de Gaulle.

3 Promenade de la Duchesse Anne

Five centuries on, the 'bonne duchesse' Anne is still remembered with affection in the town where she stayed on several occasions. It is quite conceivable that she strolled along the town walls on a summer evening, just as visitors do.
Walk through the Jardin Anglais past the Tour Ste-Catherine and down some steps into the rue du Petit-Fort. Turn right.

4 Rue du Petit-Fort

As the road leads steeply down to the river, notice on your right, at No 24, a beautiful 15th-century house. Across the Gothic bridge, the old towpath leads to the village of Léhon, 2km (1¼ miles) away, where you can see the 12th-century St-Magloire Abbey.
Retrace your steps up the rue du Petit-Fort.

5 Rue du Jerzual

Beyond the Porte du Jerzual is the cobbled rue du Jerzual. Lined with

15th-century corbelled houses, it presents the colourful scene of craftsmen at work.

Continue along the rue de la Lainerie, turn left at the place des Cordeliers and walk past the place des Merciers into the rue Haute-Voie. Turn right opposite the Ancien Hôtel Beaumanoir.

6 Basilique St-Sauveur

The basilica has a mix of architectural styles; the right side of the nave is Romanesque, the left Flamboyant Gothic. Du Guesclin's heart is said to be kept in St-Sauveur.

Walk straight to the rue de l'Horloge.

7 Rue de l'Horloge

On your right is the belfry that houses a 15th-century clock and a large bell, known as Anne, a gift from the young duchess in 1507. On your left is the Hôtel Kératry, which houses the tourist office.

Turn right into the rue Ste-Claire to return to the place du Guesclin.

Northern Brittany

Bordering the Channel from Le Mont-St-Michel Bay to Lannion, and stretching south to Rennes and Mûr-de-Bretagne, northern Brittany roughly fits within the limits of the Côtes d'Armor département, except for the short strip of coastline from Cancale to St-Malo, which belongs to Ille-et-Vilaine.

The Côtes d'Armor has the most varied coastline in Brittany.

Indented by the deep estuaries of the Rance, Trieux and Jaudy rivers, by wide bays and small creeks, the shores are scattered with huge boulders or lined with fine golden sand, and enhanced by a rainbow of colours at Côte d'Emeraude and Côte de Granit Rose. Striking scenery includes the heath on top of Cap Fréhel ablaze with golden gorse, the pink coast of Île de Bréhat, and the wild Sept Îles teeming with bird life. And twice a day strong tidal movements cause dramatic changes in the landscape.

LE CHEMIN DES PEINTRES EN CÔTE D'EMERAUDE

Between Dinard and Cap Fréhel, this unusual open-air museum exhibits some 30 faithful reproductions of famous paintings by Auguste Renoir, Émile Bernard, Pablo Picasso and others, on the spot where they were painted.

Information from local tourist offices and Comité Départemental du Tourisme, Office de Tourisme de Rennes, 11 rue St-Yves 35064 (*tel: 02 99 67 11 11*; *www.tourisme-rennes.com*).

Resorts range from fashionable Dinard to the family resorts of Perros-Guirec and Trégastel-Plage or the more modest St-Quay-Portrieux – all with beautiful beaches – while modern marinas neighbour traditional fishing harbours.

Maritime culture

The Côtes d'Armor has a rich cultural heritage: ancient fishing traditions, a turbulent past and an exceptional spirit of adventure. All this lives on through annual events such as *pardons* and folk festivals, and a new determination to use traditional ships in regattas and on commemorative occasions.

Secret Argoat

The secluded inland areas of northern Brittany are dotted with small towns of architectural interest such as Moncontour, Quintin and Jugon-les-Lacs. Here, ancient crafts live on, and a wealth of small chapels wait to be discovered by visitors.

ST-MALO

St-Malo has a population of 60,000. It is a thriving commercial and fishing harbour and has a growing ferry traffic with Britain and the Channel Islands. St-Malo is also a popular seaside resort, but it is first and foremost a historic city. Severely damaged in August 1944, it has been faithfully restored.

The Malouins (St-Malo natives) seem to have more than their fair share of the qualities and faults of ordinary Bretons: boldness, determination and a yearning for freedom. Firmly camped on their rock, they fought to keep in check the ambitions of their powerful French and English neighbours.

The city was named after a Welsh monk, Maclow, who arrived in the 6th century. Shipowners became extremely rich, pursuing St-Malo's policy of naval supremacy, while its famous corsairs kept their rivals at bay. Exasperated by the Wars of Religion during the 16th century, the city declared itself a republic until it saw fit to acknowledge the tolerant Henri IV as its lawful king.

Trade with Africa, South America and India flourished in the 17th and 18th centuries, followed by the golden age of long-distance fishing off Newfoundland and Greenland.

Natives of St-Malo include famous sailors such as Jacques Cartier, Duguay-Trouin and Surcouf, and the writer Chateaubriand (*see box*).

Fort National

Louis XIV's famous military architect, Vauban, designed Fort Royal in 1689 to reinforce the city's defences. In 1692 it withstood a combined attack by the English and Dutch fleets. The fort was renamed Fort National during the Revolution.

Open: June–Sept. Accessible on foot only at low tide. Guided tours only. For information contact the tourist office: Tel: 02 99 85 34 33; www.fortnational.com. Admission charge.

Grand Bé Island

According to his wishes, Chateaubriand was buried on this rocky island. A simple granite cross stands atop the anonymous stone under which the writer lies, facing the sea. *Accessible on foot at low tide.*

FRANÇOIS-RENÉ DE CHATEAUBRIAND (1768–1848)

Chateaubriand was an outstanding literary and political figure of his age, who towered as a writer, philosopher and man of influence – bold, sometimes unwise, always proud of his Breton heritage. In his *Mémoires d'Outre-Tombe* (Reflections Beyond the Grave), he confessed that the sea had been his first love.

A solitary child of emotionally distant parents, he nurtured his imagination for two formative years in the gloomy family castle of Combourg and in the surrounding woods.

He became a leader of the Romantic movement and, by the age of 40, had already achieved international recognition, although his masterpiece, the *Mémoires*, was yet to come.

Chateaubriand died in Paris but was buried, as he had wished, on Grand Bé Island, facing his beloved sea.

St-Malo

Paramé

The superb sheltered beach stretches from the foot of the castle to the Pointe de Rochebonne, backed by a promenade. There is a fashionable hydrotherapy centre close to the beach.

Walled city

Referred to as St-Malo *intra muros*, this is exactly what it is: completely enclosed within formidable walls. Climb the steps by the Porte St-Vincent and walk right round the fortifications. From the top you can see the narrow streets and shipowners' houses in the town; and the harbour, St-Servan, the Rance estuary, Dinard and Grand Bé Island. Near the oldest (12th century) part of the walls are the statues of Cartier and Surcouf. On the harbour side, the walls date from the 18th century.

Cathédrale St-Vincent

The cathedral was built between the 12th and 19th centuries, and restored after World War II. The luminous 13th-century chancel inside is decorated with remarkable modern stained glass.
Rue St-Benoist. Tel: 02 99 40 82 31. Open: June–Aug Mon–Sat 9.45am–7pm, Sun 9.30am–6pm; Sept–May Mon–Sat 9.45am–noon & 2–7pm, Sun 9.30–noon & 2–6pm.

Château (Musée d'Histoire de la Ville et du Pays Malouin)

This structure barred access to the city on the land side. The 15th-century Grand Donjon (Great Keep) houses a museum devoted to the history of St-Malo, while opposite it, in the Tour Quic-en-Groigne, a waxworks museum illustrates St-Malo's glorious past.
Place Chateaubriand, Grand Donjon. Tel: 02 99 40 71 57; www.saint-malo.fr. Open: Apr–Sept, daily 10am–noon & 2–6pm. Closed: Mon & public holidays in winter. Admission charge.
Quic-en-Groigne. Tel: 02 99 40 80 26. Open: daily July & Aug 9.30am–noon & 2–6pm; Apr–June & Sept–Oct 9–11.30am & 2–5.30pm. Admission charge.

Rothéneuf

On the northeastern outskirts of the town is Rothéneuf, worth a visit for its Manoir Jacques Cartier, the house where the famous explorer settled down in later life. Mainly 15th and 16th century, it is furnished in the appropriate style. A video documentary explains how Cartier discovered Canada in 1534.
Limoëlou, rue David McDonald Stewart. Tel: 02 99 40 97 73; www.musee-jacques-cartier.com. Open: July & Aug daily 10–11.30am & 2.30–6pm; June & Sept Mon–Sat 10–11.30am; Oct–May, tours at 10am & 3pm. Admission charge.

St-Servan-sur-Mer
Château du Bos

St-Malo's wealthy shipowners built country houses such as the Château du Bos in the 18th century. The reception rooms still have their original wood panelling, the library contains 6,000 books from the 19th century, and there is a beautiful collection of model ships.

In the extensive park overlooking the River Rance, four statues sculpted out of Italian marble depict the four seasons.

5km (3 miles) south of St-Servan on the N137 and the D5.
Tel: 02 99 81 40 11. Open: July & Aug, tours at 3.30pm & 5pm; June & Sept by appointment.
Admission charge.

Corniche d'Aleth

The footpath round the Aleth Peninsula affords impressive views of St-Malo, the Rance estuary, Dinard and part of the Côte d'Emeraude. On the north side is the Fort de la Cité, dating from 1759, which was one of the main defences of the 'Atlantic Wall' during World War II, with blockhouses linked by underground galleries.

Grand Aquarium

This aquarium is a great place to introduce children to the wonders of the sea. There are beautiful sea creatures on show in both underground aquaria and open-air pools. It also boasts the world's only 'nautibus' – a submarine simulator that gives visitors the feeling that they are interacting with (as opposed to observing) life beneath the waves.

Avenue de Général Patton. Tel: 02 99 21 19 00; www.aquarium-st-malo.com.
Open: daily Apr–June & Sept 10am–7pm; July & Aug 9.30am–8pm; Oct–Mar 10am–6pm.
Closed: part of Jan & Nov.
See website for detailed calendar.
Admission charge.

Tour Solidor

This impressive 14th-century tower, which faces the Rance estuary, was built (*cont on p56*)

The picturesque Tour Solidor beside the Rance

Le Mont-St-Michel

For centuries, life on the rock lying just off the coast of northern Brittany and Normandy and known as Le Mont-St-Michel was governed by the clockwork movement of the tides, for the tiny granite island was totally surrounded by the sea at high tide and only accessible at low tide. This dramatic situation, and the mysticism pertaining to its abbey, has contributed to making Le Mont-St-Michel one of the most visited places in France.

Deposits of sand are threatening to link the island to the mainland but visitors still flock to see the magnificent abbey crowning the top and witness the spectacular tidal movements which, twice a day, alter the landscape in an unforgettable way.

Legend and history

Today's visitors reach Le Mont-St-Michel by means of a 2km (1¼-mile) long causeway built in 1877, but before then thousands of pilgrims crossed the bay on foot at low tide – many perishing in the quicksands or being swept away by the fast-moving tide. However, danger did not deter them, and they kept on coming to fulfil a vow or ask a favour.

The legend began in the 8th century when Aubert, Bishop of Avranches, saw a vision of St Michael the archangel, who ordered him to build a sanctuary on the island. The sanctuary soon became a place of pilgrimage, with villages all around it.

Several buildings succeeded Bishop Aubert's modest oratory, until history took over from legend with the construction of the Romanesque abbey, replaced and extended later by superb Gothic buildings collectively known as 'La Merveille' (the Marvel).

The abbey was used as a prison for a while before and after the Revolution, but in 1874 it was entrusted to the care of the Service des Monuments Historiques.

The abbey

The heavily fortified abbey was never captured, not even during the Hundred Years' War when the English occupied the whole area. From the car park, access is gained by the Porte de l'Avancée: go up the Grande Rue through the walled town, up a series of stairs, and through an imposing gateway.

The abbey church sitting atop the mound is supported by crypts built into the rock. The steeple is surmounted by a statue of St Michael 157m (515ft) above sea level. Inside, the Flamboyant Gothic chancel is magnificent.

On the north side is the splendid Gothic ensemble built on three levels at the beginning of the 13th century, including the remarkable cloisters, where the wealth of poetic expression in the intricate yet harmonious decorations was undoubtedly stimulated by religious fervour.

The local bus service connects Le Mont-St-Michel and St-Malo.

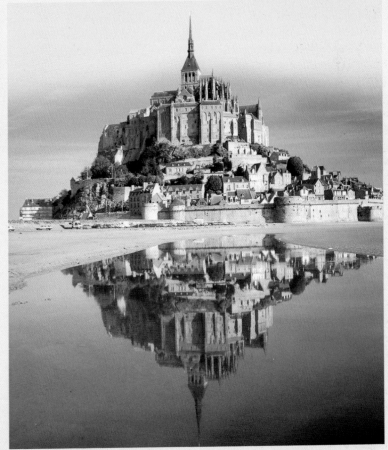

Strikingly outlined against sky and sea, Le Mont-St-Michel creates a dramatic picture by Duke Jean IV as a demonstration of strength at the end of the War of Succession, when both the English king and French king had tried to impose conditions on Brittany. It now houses the interesting Musée des Cap-Horniers, devoted to the epic voyages of the vulnerable ships that sailed round Cape Horn from the 16th century onwards. Navigation techniques, life on board and memorable events are illustrated by means of models, instruments and mementoes brought back.

Tel: 02 99 40 71 58; www.saint-malo.fr. Open: Apr–Oct Tue–Sun 10am–noon & 2–6pm. Closed: Mon & public holidays. Admission charge.

Belle-Isle-en-Terre

This quiet riverside town is set at the heart of unspoilt countryside where the narrow valleys of the Léguer and the Guic meet. It is surrounded by hills and woods with poetic names like Coat-an-Hay (Day Wood) and Coat-an-Noz (Night Wood), and is well worth discovering without the pressures of time.

Loc-Envel

The unassuming exterior of the Gothic village church does not prepare you for the wealth of decorations within. Every projecting part of the wooden vaulting is adorned with painted sculptures depicting saints, Apostles and angels, mingling with grotesque figures and fierce-looking animals. A beautiful 16th-century rood screen, a granite

altar and a stained-glass window in the chancel dating from 1540 complete this profusion of ornamentation.

4km (2¹/₂ miles) south of Belle-Isle-en-Terre by the D33.

Locmaria

Overlooking the Léguer Valley, Locmaria Chapel stands at the centre of a small cemetery. A pleasant surprise awaits you inside – a lovely 16th-century rood screen decorated with painted statues of the Apostles.

1.5km (1 mile) north of Belle-Isle-en-Terre off the D33.

Ménez-Bré

From its 302m (991ft) summit – pretty high by Breton standards – this isolated

The Gothic-Renaissance tower of Bourbriac's church points heaven-ward

'mountain' affords magnificent views extending north as far as the sea and west to the Monts d'Arrée. The chapel crowning it is dedicated to St Hervé, one of Brittany's numerous healing saints.

9km (6 miles) northeast of Belle-Isle-en-Terre off the Guingamp road.

Belle-Isle-en-Terre is 17km (11 miles) west of Guingamp.

Bourbriac

This restful country town owes its name to St Briac, who is reputed to heal nervous diseases. At its centre, the church bears witness to the generations of pilgrims who came hoping for a miracle: you can see the stone bench in the 11th-century crypt where the sick used to sit. The crossing (intersection between the nave and transept) is Romanesque, and the tower is transitional in style – the porch being Flamboyant Gothic, and the upper part Renaissance. The church contains a granite sarcophagus said to contain the remains of St Briac.

Notre-Dame d'Avaugour and Notre-Dame de Restudo

Both dating from the 14th and 15th centuries, these are typical of the many delightful chapels to be found at the heart of inland Brittany. Avaugour Chapel contains remarkable carved wooden furniture, and statues of the Twelve Apostles, while the Notre-Dame de Restudo nave and chancel have some interesting 14th-century frescoes.

7km (4 miles) east of Bourbriac, both off the D767 and 2km (1¼ miles) apart.

Bourbriac is 12.5km (8 miles) south of Guingamp on the D8.

Île de Bréhat

At the centre of an archipelago, Bréhat is surrounded by pink granite reefs glittering in the sun, around which motorboats skilfully wend their way. With a length of only 3.5km (2 miles) and 1.5km (1 mile) at its widest, Bréhat can be discovered on foot or on a bicycle – which is just as well, because cars are not allowed on the island and must be left in the free parking area at the Pointe de l'Arcouest.

The unusually mild climate accounts for the profusion of 'exotic' plants such as mimosas, eucalyptus and fig trees, and explains why hydrangea flowers brighten up the island's gardens well into October and even November.

The island's only village, known simply as Le Bourg, is in the sunnier southern part, where houses are built of local pink granite. Winding paths lead to various points on the island: St-Michel Chapel on the west coast overlooking Béniguet Island, the vast Baie de la Corderie lined with beautiful villas, and the Rosebo and Paon lighthouses in the wilder northern part of Bréhat.

The locals – just a few hundred, known as Bréhatins – are, like all Bretons, proud of their seafaring

Oyster fishermen in Cancale

traditions and will tell you that, if Christopher Columbus found his way to America, it was thanks to a fisherman from Bréhat who gave him directions!

2km (1¼ miles) off the Pointe de l'Arcouest, north of Paimpol. Access from Vedettes de Bréhat. Tel: 02 96 55 79 50; www.vedettesdebrehat.com.

For bicycle hire: tel: 02 96 20 06 26 or 02 96 20 03 51.

Bulat-Pestivien

The splendid church of this modest village points to its importance as a place of pilgrimage in the late Middle Ages. The porch is magnificent, and the Renaissance tower elegant. Inside is an imposing stone table, dating from 1583, on which offerings used to be placed.

Bulat-Pestivien also has three ancient fountains which, like many fountains in

Brittany, are associated with both Celtic and Christian rites.

22km (14 miles) southwest of Guingamp on the D787 and D31.

Cancale

To gourmets, Cancale is the name of a fine oyster, *l'huître de Cancale*, which comes from this fishing port on the shores of the Baie du Mont-St-Michel – one of the oldest, most important centres of oyster-breeding in Brittany.

Before the 18th century, oysters were plentiful in the bay and much appreciated at court. When stocks began to diminish, a royal decree restricted oyster-fishing to just a few weeks in springtime.

Oyster-breeding began in the 19th century: young oysters collected from the bay were brought back to grow and fatten in oyster beds. In the 1920s, an epidemic destroyed the supply of young oysters. Today's oysters are imported from the coast of Morbihan, and 3,000 tonnes are produced every year. Great efforts are now being made to breed young oysters again in the bay.

The town of Cancale, workaday rather than pretty, overlooks the harbour of La Houle from a plateau. If you see fishermen unload their catch, you may be tempted to buy the oysters for sale on the quayside. Or you can simply watch the fishermen's activity from one of the restaurants.

La Ferme Marine (Musée de l'Huître et du Coquillage)

This museum of oysters and seashells has a guided tour, with a video documentary on oyster-breeding and an exhibition of more than 1,500 seashells from all over the world.
'L'Aurore'. Route de la Corniche.
Tel: 02 99 89 69 99. Admission charge.

Pointe du Grouin

The path known as the Sentier des Douaniers follows the coast to Pointe du Grouin, 7km (4 miles) away; it was earlier used by customs officers to pursue smugglers. From the top of the 40m (130ft) high cliffs, you can admire the Côte d'Emeraude and Le Mont-St-Michel Abbey, or the birds on the Îles des Landes.

Cancale is 15km (9 miles) east of St-Malo on the D355.

Cap Fréhel

See p73.

Château de la Hunaudaye

In ruins but still impressive, the Château de la Hunaudaye is a striking example of what a feudal fortress was like. Even today one can imagine the sense of power its formidable towers must have given its occupants. Belonging to the influential Tournemine family, who backed the losing side in the War of Succession, it was reduced to ruins but rebuilt in the 14th and 15th centuries. Then, during

BISQUINES

Based in Cancale, these traditional fishing boats, rigged with 350sq m (3,770sq ft) of sail, were used to gather young oysters out in Le Mont-St-Michel Bay. This annual event turned into a real festival of the sea, with some 200 bisquines out in the bay at once. A replica launched in 1987, called the *Cancalaise*, is now used for pleasure trips around the bay and to the Channel Islands from mid-March to mid-November.
For information, *tel: 02 99 89 77 87; www.lacancalaise.org*

the Revolution, it was dismantled once again by the Republican army, who feared it might become a Chouan stronghold. During the summer season, life in a medieval castle is re-created by actors in period costumes.
15km (9 miles) east of Lamballe. Tel: 02 96 34 82 10; www.la-hunaudaye.com. Open: mid-June–mid-Sept daily 10.30am–6.30pm; Apr–mid-June &

Hunaudaye Castle, pillaged for stone until 1930

*mid-Sept–mid-Oct Sun & holidays
2.30–6pm. Admission charge.*

Château de Rosanbo

Little remains of the original 'rock on the (river) Bo' built in the 14th and 15th centuries. The present castle is an elegant 17th- and 18th-century manor house looking out onto French-style terraced gardens designed by Duchêne (*see p142*). Inside there are fine pieces of furniture, Aubusson and Flemish tapestries, and a library that once belonged to Louis XIV's finance minister.

Lanvellec, 20km (12 miles) southwest of Lannion on the D786 and D22. Tel: 02 96 35 18 77; www.rosanbo.net. Open: daily Apr–June & Sept 2–5pm; July & Aug 11am–6pm; Oct Sun 2–5pm. Admission charge.

Châtelaudren

See p147.

Victorian houses overlook the coast at Dinard

Dinard

Known as the 'Pearl of the Emerald Coast', Dinard became a fashionable resort in the mid-19th century, popular with American and English tourists for its fine setting and mild climate. It still retains some of its *belle époque* atmosphere.

Dinard has three lovely beaches. The deep, well-sheltered **plage de l'Écluse** is backed by luxury hotels, the casino and the Palais des Congrès. It is linked to the **plage du Prieuré** by the romantic Promenade du Clair de Lune along the Rance estuary. Facing the open sea, the **plage de St-Enogat** nestles below rocks.

Usine Marémotrice de la Rance

This impressive tidal power station, opened in 1966, harnesses the energy of both the incoming and outgoing tides of the estuary. From there, it is possible to make an interesting round trip by car to Dinan in a day.

*3km (2 miles) south on the D114. Tel: 02 99 16 37 00. Open: daily 8.30am–8pm. Free admission.
Dinard is 25km (16 miles) north of Dinan on the D266 and D766.*

Erquy

With its seven sandy beaches, Erquy was one of the first resorts to be developed along the Côte d'Emeraude, and today it is still one of the most popular. The bustling port accounts for much of its appeal. Coastal fishing is the main activity, and the return of the flotilla early in the morning is followed

Erquy's fishing boats rest by day alongside the cliffs that butt against its popular harbour

of small islands. One of them, crowned with a chapel dedicated to St Michael the Archangel, is accessible at low tide. *7.5km (5 miles) northeast of Erquy via the D786 and D34.*
Erquy is 33km (21 miles) northeast of St-Brieuc on the D786.

Guingamp

Situated between Armor and Argoat, Guingamp has no obvious tourist appeal and most people now take the bypass to reach the coast more quickly. It is a shame, though, not to go through the town and stop, if only long enough to get the feel of the place du Centre and the rue Notre-Dame, the historic heart of the city and today a lively shopping area.

Guingamp is quite modest about its past, yet it had its moments of glory when Brittany was an independent duchy. The dukes stayed in the castle here, which was dismantled in 1626 by order of Richelieu. Parts of the walls can still be seen on the place du Vally, behind the church.

Notre-Dame-de-Bon-Secours

The Gothic south tower fell down in 1535, taking part of the nave with it. A young architect, Jean Le Moal, rebuilt the south side in Renaissance style, hardly known in Brittany at the time, and decorated the west portal with a blend of religious and secular motifs. One of the most famous *pardons* takes place here in early July.
Rue Notre-Dame.

by the noisy auction of the catch in a vast open hall (*vente à la criée*). The speciality is scallops, but, as everywhere along the coast, a great variety of fresh fish is caught and sold immediately to wholesalers and restaurants. The sale takes place every day on weekdays and starts at 7am.

Cap d'Erquy

The heath-covered promontory provides shelter for Erquy's many beaches and offers panoramic views of the Baie de St-Brieuc as far as Île de Bréhat.
Cap d'Erquy is 3.5km (2 miles) northwest of Erquy.

Sables-d'Or-les-Pins

'Golden sands and pine trees' – the name itself is an invitation hard to resist. The superb beach faces a group

Place du Centre

The town's main square is shaded with trees and surrounded by 16th- and 17th-century half-timbered houses. Its triangular shape emphasises its medieval character, and the lovely off-centre Renaissance fountain completes the picture. Known as La Plomée, because it is partly made of lead, it is decorated with rams, dragons, sirens, angels and dolphins.

Nearby

Armoripark, *see p162.*

Guingamp is 30km (19 miles) northwest of St-Brieuc on the N12.

Jugon-les-Lacs

See p147.

Lamballe

See p76.

Lannion

Lannion is within easy reach of the Côte de Granit Rose and of the lovely valley of the River Léguer, famous for its excellent salmon. It's an ideal base for those who wish to sample the different facets of Brittany without driving too many miles: good bathing, superb scenery, green, undulating countryside, and a variety of typical architecture.

Lannion is now a modern telecommunications centre, but several of its tall and narrow old houses – some with corbels and pointed gables,

others with mantles of slate – still stand around the church of St-Jean-du-Baly.

Brélévenez church

The church looks down on the town from where it stands on a steep hill. It was built by the Knights Templar in the 12th century and remodelled in the 15th century. You can drive up to the church, or climb 142 granite steps leading up. Of particular interest are the Romanesque apse and the steeple with its granite spire.
Place E Laurent.

Château de Kergrist

A happy blend of styles, this castle has a Gothic north façade and an elegant 18th-century south façade in keeping with the French-style gardens.
9km (6 miles) south off the D11.
Tel: 02 96 38 91 44;
http://kergrist.monsite.wanadoo.fr.
Gardens open: mid-Apr–Oct daily

Contrasting happily, two old houses in the main square add to Lannion's Breton character

11am–6pm, tours of interior by chance or prior arrangement. Admission charge.

Château de Tonquédec

The ruins clinging to an outcrop overlooking the Léguer are a silent witness of the struggle for power and independence that tore Brittany apart for centuries. This impressive fortress was twice dismantled.

11.5km (7 miles) south on the D31B. Tel: 02 96 54 60 70; www.chateau-tonquedec.com. Open: July & Aug daily 10am–6pm; May, June & Sept weekends 10am–6pm; other times by appointment. Hours may vary each year according to caretaker's schedule, so confirm before making a special trip. Admission charge.

Léguer Valley

South of Lannion, the Léguer is a fast stream cutting its way through a narrow green valley. The 15th-century **Chapelle de Kerfons** stands like a delicately carved stone jewel in a setting of chestnut trees. The interior contains a wealth of magnificent wood carvings: a Flamboyant painted rood screen with statues of the Apostles reminiscent of St-Fiacre Chapel (*see p126*) and an ornate retable surmounted by angels.
7km (4 miles) south off the D31b.

Pointe de Séhar

A twisting road follows the south bank of the Léguer estuary through Loguivy, with its quaint parish close dedicated to St Ivy, to the Pointe de Séhar, which guards the entrance to the estuary and

offers extensive views over Lannion Bay. *Lannion is 32km (20 miles) northwest of Guingamp on the D767.*

Loudéac
See p77.

Moncontour
See p76.

Mûr-de-Bretagne

A lively market town deep at the heart of inland Brittany, Mûr-de-Bretagne is a convenient starting point for a tour of Lake Guerlédan nearby. But first have a look at the rich interior decoration of the charming Chapelle Ste-Suzanne, which inspired Corot.

Brélévenez church, Lannion

Boats of all shapes and sizes in Paimpol harbour

Lac de Guerlédan

This sinuous lake, the largest in Brittany, fits so well into its wooded surroundings that it is hard to believe it was artificially created when a dam was built across the Blavet in the 1920s.

Past the village of St-Aignan and its charming 12th-century church, a minor road cuts through the Forêt de Quénécan. Wood from the forest was used in the Rohan family's ironworks of Les Forges des Salles; their ruined castle is close to the village.

Further on, near a lock on the River Blavet, stand the ruins of the Cistercian **Abbaye de Bon Repos**. North of the river, the River Daoulas goes through a narrow gorge on its way to join the Blavet, and a pleasant shaded road runs alongside. Boat trips and watersports are available from Beau Rivage.

Mûr-de-Bretagne is 17km (11 miles) north of Pontivy on the D767.

Paimpol

Yachts and cabin cruisers are moored here today, but graceful schooners first brought fame to this town. Paimpol is known now mainly for coastal fishing and oyster-breeding, but in days gone by it was closely linked with cod-fishing. Up to 80 schooners would leave port together, bound for North Atlantic waters scattered with treacherous icebergs, and hundreds of fishermen, known as Les Islandais, died off the coasts of Newfoundland and Iceland.

The quiet of place du Martray, and its austere, stately granite houses with carved embrasures, is a marked contrast to the confusion of colourful boats in the harbour just a few steps away.

Abbaye de Beauport

Built in the 13th century close to the sea, the abbey was in use until the Revolution. Hydrangeas grow among the imposing ruins. Sound and light shows take place from 10pm to 1am every Wednesday and Sunday in July and August.

Paimpol-Kerity, 3km (2 miles) south on the D786. Tel: 02 96 55 18 58; www.abbaye-beauport.com. Open: daily mid-June–mid-Sept 10am–7pm; mid-Sept–mid-June 10am–noon & 2–5pm. Admission charge.

Loguivy

Set amid pink granite rocks, this pretty lobster-fishing village has inspired writers and painters.

5km (3 miles) north on the D15.

Musée de la Mer

This maritime museum traces the history of fishing off the coast of Iceland. In addition, the museum hosts temporary expositions concerning nautical life (a recent theme was 'women of the coast') and exhibits the work of individual artists.

Museum: rue de la Benne. Tel: 02 96 22 02 19; www.museemerpaimpol.com. Open: daily mid-June–Aug 10.30am–12.30pm & 2–6.30pm; mid-Apr–mid-June & early Sept 2–6pm. Admission charge.

Pointe de l'Arcouest

On the way down to the vast parking area are remarkable views of the sea scattered with islets and reefs. The island of Bréhat (*see p57*), glittering in the distance, is a ten-minute ferry ride away.

9km (6 miles) north on the D789. Ferry shuttle service to Bréhat every hour.

Paimpol is 45km (28 miles) north of St-Brieuc by the D786.

Perros-Guirec

See p74.

Plestin-les-Grèves

Close to one of the best beaches on the north coast is the pleasant holiday resort of Plestin-les-Grèves, which offers exciting possibilities of excursions. The church contains the grave of St Efflam, a 5th-century Irish missionary.

The magnificent beach of Lieue de Grève, just 3km (2 miles) northeast, is at least 4km (2½ miles) long. The sea withdraws over a distance of 2km (1¼ miles) twice a day, to the immense delight of children and cockle-gatherers.

At the western end of the beach is the **Chapelle de St-Efflam**, which marks the spot where the holy man landed.

Corniche de l'Armorique

Beyond St-Efflam begins the indented Corniche de l'Armorique, well worth exploring as far as Locquirec. From the Pointe de Plestin there is a splendid view of the Lieue de Grève. Beyond, the road skirts a stream and leads to the

charming fishing port and family resort of Locquirec.
West along the D42 and D64.

Plestin-les-Grèves is 18km (11 miles) southwest of Lannion on the D786.

Pontrieux

Pontrieux developed as a bridge town at the head of the Trieux estuary and as a safe port of call for merchant ships. But eventually the town found itself too far from the sea and, having outlived its usefulness, its growth came to an end. The result is a delightful small town with a wealth of domestic architecture from the 16th to the 19th centuries.

Château de la Roche-Jagu

This fully restored 15th-century castle defended the River Trieux 60m (197ft) below, no doubt very effectively, as you can see if you follow the watchman's round on the riverside.

The charming town of Pontrieux

The interior gives a good idea of life in a medieval castle, with metre-thick walls and numerous massive fireplaces.
6km (4 miles) north off the D787.
Tel: 02 96 95 62 35. Open: daily
July & Aug 10am–1pm & 2–7pm;
Sept–June 10am–1pm.
Admission charge.

Pontrieux is 17km (11 miles) north of Guingamp on the D787.

Quintin
See p77.

St-Brieuc
St-Brieuc is both a historic town and the modern administrative and commercial centre of the *département* of Côtes d'Armor, with regular markets and trade fairs.

The city was founded in the 5th century by Brieuc, a Welsh monk and one of the seven founders of Brittany. A 15th-century fountain in the rue Ruffelet marks the place where Brieuc built his monastery. In medieval times pilgrims flocked to the town, which was on the route of the Tro Breiz (holy tour of Brittany).

The town was attacked and destroyed during the War of Succession, the Wars of Religion and the Chouan rebellion, and unfortunately little of the old town has survived. Most of the remaining old corbelled houses are to be found in the picturesque streets north of the cathedral: the rue Fardel leading to the place du Lin, the rue Quinquaine, rue du Parc and rue du Gouët (the deposed James II of England lodged here in 1689).

Cathédrale
Dating from the 13th and 14th centuries, the massive fortified edifice bears witness to the city's troubled past. From the front it looks like a medieval castle, its twin towers reinforced by buttresses and defended by machicolations. The lofty nave was rebuilt in the 18th century. Notice the beautiful stained-glass window in the south transept and the Renaissance organ loft.
Place du Général de Gaulle.

North of St-Brieuc and the River Gouët, cliffs and beaches alternate along the coast. From the **Pointe du Roselier**, rising 70m (230ft) above sea level, the view extends across the wide bay of St-Brieuc and south to the **Anse d'Yffiniac**, where the tide sometimes recedes over 7km (4 miles), revealing clusters of black mussels clinging to thick wooden posts.

Further north, there are two lovely and safe beaches, **Martin-Plage** and **Les Rosaires**, the latter 2km (1¼ miles) long.

Binic, once an important port connected with cod-fishing in the North Atlantic, is today a charming seaside resort with three good beaches and a large marina.
St-Brieuc is 99km (62 miles) northwest of Rennes on the N12.

St-Nicolas-du-Pélem

St-Nicolas is situated in the upper valley of the Blavet and is an area of considerable scenic beauty. Woods, chaotic groupings of boulders, streams and lakes make it ideal touring country for those who like the peace and quiet of minor roads and small villages.

In the chancel of the 15th- and 16th-century church are two lovely stained-glass windows depicting the Passion. Alongside the church is a charming 17th-century fountain, named after the patron saint of the village.

Gorges de Toul-Goulic

The River Blavet disappears with a thundering noise under a tumble of huge boulders in wooded surroundings. *9.5km (6 miles) northwest of St-Nicolas on the D50 and D87. The site is a 10-minute walk from the car park.*

Kergrist-Moëlou

The imposing Gothic church is out of proportion with the modest size of the village. The south side is richly decorated; 500-year-old yews and an impressive calvary complete the picture. Dating from 1578, the calvary was partly destroyed in 1793; a closer inspection reveals that some of the characters were repositioned incorrectly. *17km (11 miles) west of St-Nicolas on the D87.*

St-Nicolas is 44km (27 miles) southwest of St-Brieuc on the D790.

The chapel in St-Quay-Portrieux

St-Quay-Portrieux

You would think that a modern family seaside resort like St-Quay – with its superb bathing, brand new harbour, fun and entertainment for all ages – would surely not be linked with legend. But you wouldn't be in Brittany if there were no legend attached to the place.

The town was named after an Irish monk called Ké, who arrived a long time ago in a stone trough. Beaten by

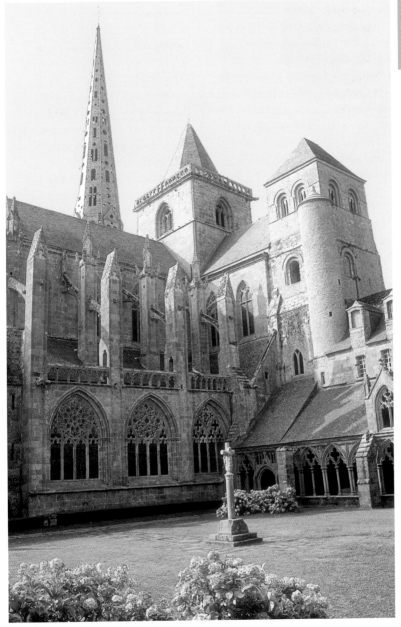

St-Tugdual Cathedral, one of the finest in Brittany

local women and left badly wounded on the shore, he prayed for help, and was healed, finding refuge under a gigantic bramble bush.

When the chapel built on the spot was destroyed in 1875, a huge bramble was found under the altar. All Bretons will assure you that the story was passed on to them by their great-grandmother, who heard it from an eyewitness!

You can walk along the Sentier des Douaniers, which follows the coast from the harbour to the plage du Châtelet, for good views of the Bay of St-Brieuc.

Côte du Goëlo

Northwest of St-Quay-Portrieux, the coast is a succession of cliffs and creeks, like the picturesque Port-Moguer. Allied aircrews, shot down over France during World War II, escaped back to Britain from the plage Bonaparte.

Kermaria-an-Iskuit

In the chapel, a realistic 15th-century Dance of Death, depicting the living holding hands with the dead, is said to have prompted Saint-Saëns to compose his *Danse Macabre*.
11.5km (7 miles) northwest of St-Quay.

St-Quay-Portrieux is 18km (11 miles) north of St-Brieuc.

Tréguier

The city has a number of old houses dating from the 15th to 18th centuries,

including philosopher Ernest Renan's birthplace, but the city's main claim to fame is the magnificent cathedral which dominates the centre of the old town.

Founded by St Tugdual, one of Brittany's seven founders, the town developed within the Jaudy estuary and soon became a powerful bishopric and an important centre of learning. But, curiously enough, its strongest associations are with another saint: Yves, a lawyer, a priest and an advocate of the poor, who lived in the 13th century and is still honoured every year in May in one of the most important *pardons* in Brittany.

Cathédrale St-Tugdual

This splendid pink granite building radiates a strong spirituality unaltered by the passing of time. It is, essentially, an imposing Gothic edifice dating from the 14th and 15th centuries; all that remains of the Romanesque cathedral is Hastings Tower over the north transept, while the spire on the south tower is 18th-century.

To the north of the nave is St Yves' tomb, dating from the 19th century, a copy of the medieval tomb destroyed during the Revolution. In the south transept is a statue of the saint between the rich and the poor, and 46 beautiful Renaissance stalls in the chancel.

Under the Romanesque arches of Hastings Tower, a door leads to the beautifully preserved Flamboyant cloister. In the vestry, you can see the relic of St Yves, which traditionally leads the procession during the famous *pardon*.

Port-Blanc

A pleasant seaside resort with a wide beach, sand dunes and an interesting 16th-century Gothic chapel.
9km (6 miles) northwest on the D70 and D74.

Tréguier is 29km (18 miles) north of Guingamp on the D8.

Le Val-André

This popular resort has one of the finest beaches on the north coast. You can see birds nesting on the island sanctuary of Le Verdelet, off the Pointe de Pléneuf and accessible at low tide.

Château de Bienassis

This fortified castle dating from the 15th and 17th centuries, complete with moat and crenellated wall, is still inhabited.
7km (4 miles) northeast off the D786. Tel: 02 96 72 22 03; www.chateau-bienassis.com. Open: mid-June–mid-Sept 10.30am–12.30pm & 2–6.30pm; other times by appointment. Closed: Sun morning. Admission charge.

Le Val-André is 26km (16 miles) northeast of St-Brieuc on the D786.

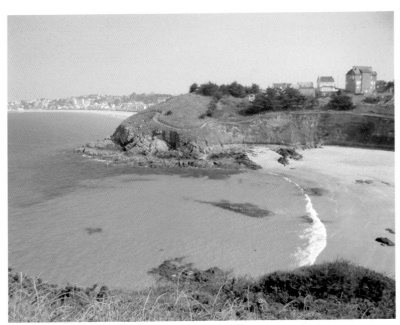

The glorious beach at Le Val-André

Tour: Côte d'Emeraude

This tour includes one of the most famous landmarks in Brittany, as well as seaside resorts, beaches, promontories and, as a contrast, the ancient walled town of Dinan.

Allow a full day.

Start from Dinard (see p60) and follow the D786 west.

1 St-Lunaire

This fashionable resort lies at the base of a tiny peninsula with a lovely beach on either side. The tip of the peninsula is known as the Pointe du Décollé; linked to the rest by a natural bridge, it offers striking views.
Continue along the D786.

2 St-Briac-sur-Mer

St-Briac is a different kind of resort, with a lively yet relaxed atmosphere, a traditional fishing harbour, a marina and lovely beaches.
Coming out of St-Briac, follow the cliff road to the new bridge across the Frémur, which has views of the resort; after 7km (4 miles), turn right on the D26.

3 St-Jacut-de-la-Mer

This fishing village and resort is camped on a narrow peninsula jutting out into the bay, with a fine beach and a cliff near the tip. Île Ebihens lies just beyond.
Double back to rejoin the D786 (which you will leave again a few kilometres

further on), past the Arguenon estuary; look for the bouchots à moules *(wooden posts used for mussel-breeding). Turn right on the D19.*

4 St-Cast-le-Guildo

St-Cast is one of the main resorts along the coast, ideally situated between two rocky promontories sheltering a curved beach. From the Pointe de St-Cast to the north there are panoramic views of the Côte d'Emeraude.
Leave St-Cast along the D13 towards Matignon, where you turn right; the road skirts the Baie de la Frênaye. Turn right onto the D341/D16.

5 Fort la Latte

About 60m (200ft) above the pounding waves, this medieval castle faces the open sea, dominating the cliff top. A path leading to the entrance passes a slim Neolithic menhir and continues on to two drawbridges spanning deep crevices. The massive round keep stands on a rocky mound inside the second courtyard. The view extends east as far as St-Malo.

Tel: 02 96 41 57 11; www.castlelalatte.com. Open: daily July & Aug 10am–7pm; Apr–June & Sept 10am–12.30pm & 2.30–6pm; weekend afternoons at other times of the year. Admission charge.

Drive northwest to Cap Fréhel.

6 Cap Fréhel

This is one of the most famous sights in Brittany, with breathtaking scenery unfolding from the edge of the 70m (230ft) high cliff. Colonies of sea birds nest on the rock face and whirl round with deafening shrieks. Go to the very tip of the promontory, beyond the lighthouse; then follow a path down to a terrace to observe the birds at close range. *Follow the scenic D34a across the heath and turn left after 5km (3 miles) to rejoin the D786. Turn left again, then right at Matignon and follow the D794 to Dinan (see pp46–7). Drive north along the D766 to return to Dinard.*

Tour: The Corniche Bretonne

Strangely shaped pink rock formations with even stranger names are the attraction along this stretch of coastline. The tour is only 30km (19 miles) long but shouldn't be rushed: there's a great deal of pleasure awaiting you on a stroll round the municipal park in Ploumanac'h, a walk from Trégastel across to Île Renote, or round the moors of Île Grande.

Allow half a day.

Start from Perros-Guirec.

1 Perros-Guirec

This is an ideal family resort, with sheltered shallow beaches particularly safe for children, a sophisticated hydrotherapy centre and plenty of entertainment, including a casino. It is also a good central base from which to explore the Côte de Granit Rose, or to take a boat trip round the Sept Îles bird sanctuary. The church is quite interesting inside: the first part of the nave is Romanesque with round pillars that are plain on the left, decorated with engaged columns on the right, and surmounted by capitals carved with Celtic motifs.
Leave Perros-Guirec by the D788 towards Ploumanac'h.

2 Ploumanac'h

A path runs along the beach where St Guirec landed in the 6th century (there is a small oratory nearby), then disappears through huge pink boulders and enters the municipal park. Follow the path round until you reach the Château du Diable, which looks like a forbidding ruined castle, then turn right to return to the car park.
Continue on the D788.

3 Trégastel-Plage

The setting of this small resort is memorable: fine sand beaches are backed by huge, wind-eroded boulders (some with individual names), while the sea is scattered with small islands. Let your imagination run free when you look at the 'Witch' or 'Death's Head' or the 'Pile of Pancakes', but don't worry about the precariously perched 'Die' – it's been like that for literally ages. A narrow sandbank links the Île Renote to the mainland, with more rocks piled chaotically.
Turn south towards Trébeurden. About 1.5km (1 mile) further on, turn left, then right to reach the Dolmen de Kerguntuil, which has an interesting covered passage. Return to the main road and continue south. The coast is particularly attractive

until Penvern; from there you could make a detour to Île Grande, which is covered with wild moors.

4 Trébeurden

This popular seaside resort has several south-facing beaches. Walk to Le Castel for good views of the coast and of the Île Milliau (accessible on foot at low tide, otherwise by boat), with a wealth of flora and fauna. Further south, the Pointe de Bihit offers a view of the Baie de Lannion and a beach below.

Drive east on the D6 to Pleumeur-Bodou and turn left.

5 Pleumeur-Bodou Radôme

Since 1962, when the first ever transatlantic TV broadcast was received here via Telstar, this huge white ball, 64m (210ft) in diameter, has been an important centre of satellite communications. Next door, a museum illustrates the history of telecommunications. There is also a vast planetarium showing ten different programmes at fixed times.

Pleumeur-Bodou Radôme. Tel: 02 96 46 63 81. Open: Apr–Sept 10am–6pm; July & Aug 10am–7pm and during school holidays. Admission charge. For further information, contact Musée des Télécommunications, www.leradome.com.

Planetarium de Bretagne.
Tel: 02 96 15 80 30 or 80 32 for details.

Continue a little further on the road to Penvern to admire a huge standing stone, the Menhir de St-Uzec, surmounted by a crucifix. Return to Pleumeur-Bodou and turn left on the D6, which takes you back to Perros-Guirec.

Tour: Ancient towns of central Brittany

This tour takes you through the heart of Argoat – inland Brittany – with its forests, undulating hills and solitary heaths. Above all, you are introduced to its small, peaceful towns.

Allow a full day.

Leave St-Brieuc on the N12 going east.

1 Lamballe

This former capital of the Duchy of Penthièvre played a considerable political role until the Revolution – and sometimes had to pay dearly for it. It was saved from economic decline by the Haras National (National Stud Farm), founded in 1825; it keeps 400 horses.
Place du Champ de Foire. Tel: 02 96 50 06 98; www.haraspatrimoine.com. Guided tours at 3pm, in English by appointment. Closed Mon. Free admission. Follow the D768 south.

2 Moncontour

A mark of Moncontour's prosperous past as a centre of the hemp and linen industry are the superb houses of merchants and craftsmen round the place de Penthièvre and in the rues du Temple and des Dames. The 16th-century church of St-Mathurin is beautifully lit by six fine stained-glass windows, inspired by Flemish artists.
Take the D6 towards Collinée and turn left after 3km (2 miles) along the D25.

3 Château de la Touche-Trébry

The castle stands in a secluded spot between a wood and a lake. Surrounded by a moat, it looks feudal although it was built in the late 16th century.
Tel: 02 96 42 78 55. Open: July–mid-Sept 2–6pm. Closed: Sun. Admission charge. Rejoin the main road and drive to Collinée, then turn right on the D792, cross the N164 and continue on the D1.

4 La Trinité-Porhoët

A fine Romanesque-Gothic church graces this sleepy little town nestling in the valley of the Ninian. The beautiful church portal is framed by slender columns with delicately carved capitals.
Follow the road to Loudéac, stopping at La Chèze to visit the captivating regional museum of Breton crafts – Musée Régional des Métiers (tel: 02 96 26 63 16; metiers.musee@wanadoo.fr; open: 10am–noon & 2–6pm; closed: Tue & public holidays; admission charge).

5 Loudéac

Loudéac is an important market town, but it's also well known for its horse-racing events in spring. The Église St-Nicolas, rebuilt in the 18th century, contains an unusual main altar set beneath a baldachin (canopy).
Drive north on the D700, then bear left on the D7 to Quintin.

6 Quintin

In the 17th and 18th centuries, Quintin experienced a sudden boom through its linen trade. Today, the town presents an architectural harmony of stately houses rising in terraces above the river. The castle is in two parts: the first part (17th century) remains unfinished; the second (18th century) houses a museum of local history (*tel: 02 96 74 04 63; open: May–Sept daily 2–5pm, longer in summer; Oct–Apr Sat & Sun 2–5pm; admission charge*).

The Notre-Dame Basilica, rebuilt in the late 19th century on the site of the previous church, contains a precious relic brought back from Jerusalem by Crusaders in 1252: a fragment of a belt said to have belonged to the Virgin Mary.
The D790 and D700 take you back to St-Brieuc.

Fishing and oyster-breeding

One of the main attractions of Brittany is its many fishing ports. The drone of diesel engines signals returning craft and heralds a sudden burst of activity. Fishermen in yellow oilskins bustle about the decks, selling the day's catch right on the quay. Locals make judicious remarks, auctions proceed noisily in over-crowded halls. In the mid-afternoon lull, brightly coloured boats bob gently with the breeze.

Best of all, as you stroll along in the quiet of the evening, is the irresistible smell of grilled fish coming from small quayside restaurants. But, of course, such an appealing picture is founded on a way of life.

Seawater in their veins

Every Breton is a fisherman at heart, ready to defy the hardships and dangers of looking for cod off the coasts of Newfoundland and Iceland, for tuna in the Indian Ocean, and for lobster off the coasts of Portugal, Morocco and even Brazil. These ever-longer voyages coincided with the development of preservation techniques. Today, most large ports

Flat-bottomed boat used for oysters and mussels

A fine specimen in Concarneau's fish market

specialise in what is called 'industrial' fishing. Concarneau sends floating factories to fish for tuna off the coast of Africa, while Douarnenez, Audierne and Camaret-sur-Mer specialise in lobster-fishing. Along the north coast, St-Malo is the only port to uphold the tradition of cod-fishing off the coast of Canada, since Paimpol and neighbouring ports have turned to scallop-fishing in St-Brieuc Bay. But smaller ports continue the ancient daily pattern of netting a variety of local fish, supplying the needs of discerning palates of native and visitor alike.

Farming the seabed

Brittany is a major source of shellfish, particularly oysters. There are two kinds: the native flat oysters and the less refined Portuguese or Japanese oysters, which were imported when an epidemic killed the majority of native oysters.

Oyster-breeding began in Brittany more than 150 years ago. The technique involves covering tiles with lime and laying them in sheltered bays or river estuaries to attract young oysters. Later these are transferred to oyster-beds (*parcs à huîtres*) until they mature three or four years later. They are then sold or placed in specific places, such as the Bélon estuary, to improve their taste. The particular balance of fresh water and sea water in the River Bélon results in the highly acclaimed flavour.

Finistère

The westernmost of Brittany's four départements has a strong sense of its own identity, evolved over the centuries from the close relationship between the people and their natural environment. Bretons have fought an ongoing duel with the elements, to achieve survival while making a living out of the sea.

The names given to some of the most dangerous spots – such as the Baie des Trépassés (Bay of the Dead) or Nouveau Cimetière (New Cemetery) – reveal the people's fear of their ancient adversary, but imply as well an acceptance of the risks involved in their way of life, which they readily defend. For the people of Finistère (the name derives from *finis terrae* – land's end) have had a long-standing love affair with the sea. They mourn their dead and curse the cruel sea, but generation after generation has answered its call.

Finistère confronts the sea on three sides, and its irregular coastline points to the struggle in which wind and waves endlessly reshape the land. To the north there are sand beaches, dunes and *abers* (shallow estuaries invaded by the sea at high tide but looking like mudflats at low tide). The west coast bears the brunt of the Atlantic's assault. Its cliffs have crumbled into the sea, forming a scatter of dark shiny reefs, and a succession of peninsulas and promontories face barren, austere islands that are often hidden in mist. Treacherous navigation has resulted in this part of Brittany having the highest concentration of lighthouses in France.

Finistère's south coast is far more welcoming. Sheltered harbours and sunny coves hint at the long sandy beaches found in Morbihan and Loire-Atlantique further south and east.

Rugged land, strong convictions

Inland Finistère has more variety than any other part of Brittany. Besides its rivers, green valleys and forests, it has in its centre the only Breton mountains – mere hills by ordinary standards, but so rugged and austere that one quickly forgets their modest height. It is here, surrounded by uncompromising nature, that the Breton temperament was inspired to a corresponding religious fervour unmatched elsewhere in Brittany, and the result can be seen in its unique parish closes (*see pp98–9*).

Finistère has guarded its Breton culture even more jealously than other parts of Brittany. Fishing is still the main occupation – and the main political issue – along the coastal fringe, which has two of the largest fishing ports in France (Douarnenez and Concarneau) as well as a string of smaller ones, like Guilvinec.

More people speak the Breton language here than anywhere else, and lifestyles are most strongly rooted in the past. Cornouaille, the southwestern part of Finistère, has been known as the bastion of traditional Brittany since the 19th century, when painters such as Paul Gauguin found inspiration in the landscapes and its people.

Finistère

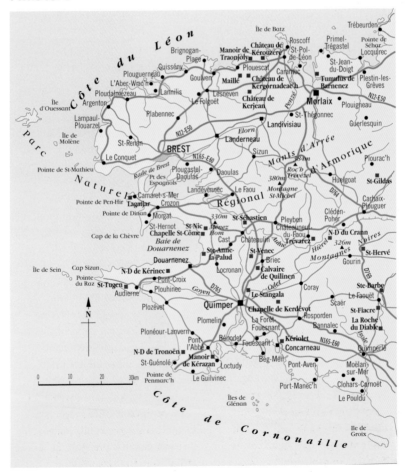

Finistère

QUIMPER

Back in the 5th or 6th century, upriver from the Gallo-Roman settlement of Aquilonia, Bretons chose the confluence of the Odet and Steir rivers as the site for their new city; this location also determined its name (*kemper* means confluence).

Gradlon, legendary 6th-century ruler of the drowned city of Ys and first King of Cornouaille, is supposed to have made Quimper his new capital, with his friend Corentin as its first bishop. The town walls and the cathedral were erected in the 13th century, but the city really began to develop during the Revolution, when it became the administrative centre of Finistère.

Today, Quimper carries out its dual role of administrative centre and ancient capital with a great deal of inventiveness. Its exceptional architectural heritage blends harmoniously with new creations such as the Halles (market hall) at the heart of the old quarter and the Maison du Département (county hall) on the River Odet. Far from being a museum piece, Quimper bustles with the excitement of a modern city, its streets suddenly swelling at lunchtime with business people. Yet, more than any other town, it seems imbued with Breton culture, symbolised by the elegant granite spires of the cathedral soaring majestically above old timber-framed houses.

From Mont-Frugy, a small hill on the south bank of the Odet, there are lovely

Quimper is situated 220km (137 miles) west of Rennes and 250km (155 miles) northwest of Nantes and connected by fast dual carriageway; 100km (62 miles) south of Roscoff, linked by ferry to Plymouth and Cork. Direct rail link to Paris by TGV (fast train). Daily flights from Paris to Quimper Pluguffan Airport; regular flights from Cork from April to September.

Office de Tourisme: *Place de la Résistance. Tel: 02 98 53 04 05; www.quimper-tourisme.com. Open: July & Aug Mon–Sat 9am–7pm, Sun 10am–12.45pm & 3–5.45pm; Sept–June Mon–Sat 9.30am–12.30pm & 1.30–6pm, Sun 10am–12.45pm.*

views of this 'City of Art' nestled in its steep-sided valley.

Cathédrale St-Corentin

This fine, imposing building dates from the 13th and 15th centuries. In 1239 it was decided to replace the existing Romanesque cathedral and work began on the chancel, but war and lack of funds delayed its completion until 1410. The nave and the towers are 15th century, but the spires were added in 1856 and modelled on that of Notre-Dame-de-Roscudon in Pont-Croix (*see p87*). If you stand back from the cathedral, you will see between the towers an equestrian statue of King Gradlon – a typically Breton link between religion and legend. Walk round to the north side to admire the flying buttresses and the porch.

Inside you will immediately notice that the nave is not in alignment with the chancel; this is probably due to technical difficulties during construction. The 15th-century stained glass of the upper windows is remarkable. The pulpit, dating from 1679, is decorated with scenes from St Corentin's life, and the organ, from 1643, is by Robert Dallam, an English organ-maker of some repute.

Musée des Beaux-Arts

Situated on the north side of the cathedral, the recently renovated Fine Arts Museum is one of the finest of its kind outside Paris. Two rooms on the ground floor are devoted to Breton paintings of the 19th century, including *Une Noce en Bretagne* (Breton Wedding) by Leleux and *Champ de Foire à Quimper* (Fairground in Quimper) by Perrin. Another room is devoted to Max Jacob, a native of Quimper, and his friends Picasso, Cocteau and others.

The extensive collection of Breton paintings continues on the first floor with the Pont-Aven School, including *Études de Bretonnes* (Breton Women) by Émile Bernard, *La Vieille du Pouldu* (Old Woman from Le Pouldu) by Sérusier and *Paysage de Pont-Aven* (Landscape from Pont-Aven) by Maufra. The Nabis and Symbolists are also represented; notice, in particular, *Pardon en Pays Bigouden* (*Pardon* in Bigouden Country) by Lionel Floch. The 20th century is represented by Delaunay, Marquet, Derain and many others; particularly striking is the life-size reconstruction of the dining room of the

Finistère

The cathedral's spires soar above the town

Hôtel de l'Épée in Quimper, decorated with Breton scenes by Jean-Julien Lemordant between 1905 and 1909.

Other rooms on the first floor contain Italian paintings from the 14th to the 18th centuries, Dutch and Flemish paintings of the 17th and 18th centuries, including works by Rubens and Jordaens, as well as a vast collection of French paintings from the 17th to the 19th centuries, including famous works by Boucher, Fragonard, Corot and Boudin. *40 place St-Corentin. Tel: 02 98 95 45 20; www.musee-beauxarts.quimper.fr. Open: July & Aug 10am–7pm; Sept–June 10am–noon & 2–6pm. Closed: Tue all year & Sun morning Nov–Mar. Admission charge.*

St-Corentin Cathedral has a number of stunning stained-glass windows from the 15th century

Musée Départemental Breton

Created in 1846, the museum is now in the old bishop's palace, between the cathedral and the river. A veritable treasure, it is devoted to Brittany's past, featuring archaeological collections with a section on prehistory and the Gallo-Roman period, and various items illustrating Breton religious art from the 12th to 17th centuries, including some painted wooden statues. There are also beautiful regional costumes, furniture and, last but not least, a unique collection of Quimper ceramics (*see p154*) from the 18th century to the present day. *1 rue du Roi Gradlon. Tel: 02 98 95 21 60. Open: June–Sept 9am–6pm; Oct–May 9am–noon & 2–5pm. Closed: Mon & Sun morning (in Oct, closed on Tue). Admission charge.*

Musée de la Faïence

The Ceramics Museum traces 300 years of pottery-making in Quimper (*see p154*).

A vast collection of more than 2,000 pieces, shown in rotation, are decorated with religious and historical themes, scenes of daily life or abstract motifs. The items exhibited illustrate the evolution of the craft and the blending of famous styles from other French regions such as Rouen, Nevers and Moustiers. The manufacturing process is clearly explained with samples of the tools and raw materials used. *14 rue J B Bousquet. Tel: 02 98 90 12 72; www.quimper-faiences.com. Open: mid-Apr–mid-Oct 10am–6pm. Closed: Sun. Admission charge.*

Nearby you can also tour the workshop of Faïenceries de Quimper H B Henriot; guided tours are available in French and English, and the curious can try their hand at special workshops by reservation. *Rue Haute. Tel: 02 98 90 09 36, 08 00 62 65 10 for tour schedule (free call); www.hb-henriot.com. Open: Mon–Fri, Mon–Sat in July & Aug. Closed: Sun. Admission charge.*

Notre-Dame-de-Locmaria

Standing on the south bank of the River Odet, this Romanesque church was part of a Benedictine monastery. The interior is quite bare apart from a rood beam bearing Christ wrapped in a robe.

Nearby
Chapelle de Kerdévot

This beautifully located 15th-century chapel contains a Flemish retable which tells the story of the Virgin Mary. *8km (5 miles) east of Quimper on the D15.*

Quilinen and St-Venec calvaries

These two calvaries were undoubtedly carved by the same craftsmen, for they both have an unusual triangular base. This device allows the statues to be placed on different levels, thus naturally drawing the eye upwards to the top of the cross. *8km (5 miles) north off the D770 and 5km (3 miles) further on the same road.*

Site du Stangala

From the parking area, a path leads through the woods right to a natural terrace which overlooks – from a height of 80m (262ft) – a bend in the River Odet. *6km (4 miles) north on a minor road branching off the D15 to Coray on the left.*

Les Abers

The low-lying coastal area of northwest Finistère is known as the Pays des Abers (*aber* country) because its rocky

Cafés and shops line the pedestrianised streets of Quimper

coastline is punctuated with estuaries called *abers*. Nothing like the deep Rance or Trieux estuaries of the north coast, they are in fact the shallow outlets of small streams. A common sight is the many small boats left stranded in the mud at low tide.

The sea here is scattered with reefs, and navigating can be tricky in spite of the numerous lighthouses. However, several picturesque harbours such as L'Aber-Wrac'h, Portsall, Porspoder and Lanildut still pursue age-old activities, essentially local fishing and the gathering of *goémon* (seaweed) used as a fertiliser. Particularly plentiful in this area, you can see it drying on the sand dunes of Ste-Marguerite Peninsula, between L'Aber-Wrac'h and L'Aber Benoît, which has lovely views of both.

Further south, a pretty road follows the coast closely between Trémazan and Argenton; here you can see the

notorious Roches de Portsall, on which the oil tanker *Amoco Cadiz* ran aground in 1978, causing the worst pollution ever seen on the coast of Brittany.

Audierne

Situated at the entrance of the Goyen estuary, Audierne is today a medium-size fishing port specialising in lobster and crawfish; the catch is stocked in seawater pools that can be visited. Some of the large trawlers that used to fish off the coasts of Portugal, Morocco and even Brazil now rest in a ships' graveyard on the banks of the River Goyen.

Île de Sein

This unassuming patch of flat land, at the mercy of the ocean's wrath, is steeped in legend – no doubt because a ring of treacherous reefs and violent currents make for difficult access. In Celtic times it was the final resting place of the mystical Druids, but for generations now it has been home to fishermen and their families.

On the western side of the island, the sea is so rough that the Ar Men lighthouse, which stands on an isolated reef, took 30 years to build at the end of the 19th century. The island entered French history books in 1940, when the entire male population crossed the Channel to join General de Gaulle's Free French Army in Britain.

23km (14 miles) west of Audierne. Regular boat service from Audierne-Ste-Evette; sailing time 1 hour. No cars allowed.

Coastal routes in Finistère are dotted with lovely stone churches

Lighthouse at Bénodet

Pont-Croix

This ancient market town is famous for its 13th-century church, **Notre-Dame-de-Roscudon**, whose splendid architecture has had a long-lasting influence: centuries later, its 67m (220ft) spire was the model for those of St-Corentin Cathedral in Quimper. Most remarkable is the south porch, with its three delicately carved gables.

Decorated like an olden-days Breton home, **Le Marquisat** museum is a fascinating glimpse into the past.
5.5km (3 miles) northeast of Audierne on the D765.

Le Marquisat. Tel: 02 98 70 51 86; www.chez.com/pontcroix. Open: daily July & Aug 10.30am–12.30pm & 3.30–6.30pm; June & Sept 3–6pm; Oct–May Sun & holidays 3–6pm.

Audierne is 36km (22 miles) west of Quimper on the D784.

Bénodet

This elegant seaside resort at the entrance of the Odet estuary has three beaches, a casino and a vast marina packed with yachts. From the centre, the avenue de Kercréven leads to a wooded area overlooking the harbour, the estuary and the pretty Pont de Cornouaille. From the bridge are striking views of Bénodet harbour and Ste-Marine opposite.

Nearby

The tiny hamlet of **Le Letty** lies on the shores of the peaceful laguna called Mer Blanche, ideal for safe sailing (instruction available).
4km (2¹/₂ miles) on the D44 east and minor road south.

Bénodet is 15km (9 miles) south of Quimper; boat trips upriver to Quimper and to Îles de Glénan.

Brest

Brest is undoubtedly the most prestigious of French ports, associated with the country's maritime history from the colourful days of the Royale (French navy of historical times) to the

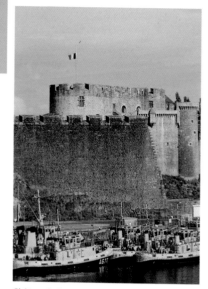

Château in Brest

From the castle, the cours Dajot, on the old town walls, affords views of the whole harbour.
Tel: 02 98 22 12 39; www.mairie-brest.fr. Open: Apr–mid-Sept daily 10am–6.30pm; mid-Sept–mid-Dec & Feb–Mar Wed–Mon 10am–noon & 2–6pm. Closed: mid-Dec–Jan. Admission charge.

Musée des Beaux-Arts

The most interesting exhibits of this Fine Arts Museum are the works of painters of the Pont-Aven School, including Émile Bernard and Paul Sérusier.
29 rue Traverse. Tel: 02 98 00 87 96; www.mairie-brest.com. Open: Tue–Sat 10am–noon & 2–6pm, Sun 2–6pm. Closed: Mon. Admission charge.

Océanopolis

This oceanographic centre, resembling a giant architectural crab, takes you on a journey into the ocean's depths with the help of huge aquariums, the largest in Europe. Plan for at least half a day and go early in high season.
Port de Plaisance du Moulin Blanc. Tel: 02 98 34 40 40; www.oceanopolis.com. Open: Apr–Aug daily 9am–6pm; Sept–Mar Tue–Sat 10am–5pm, Sun 10am–6pm. Closed: Mon off-season & Christmas–New Year. Admission charge.

Pont de Recouvrance

An impressive piece of engineering, the bridge has a main span of 87m (285ft)

more sombre events of World War II, when the city was totally destroyed.

The new town has wide avenues and vast open spaces and is once again France's major naval port on the Atlantic. Its shipyards build the largest warships in France, such as the aircraft carrier *Charles de Gaulle*, the latest to be launched. In addition, Brest has taken on the new roles of university town and oceanographic research centre.

Château and Musée de la Marine

Situated at the mouth of the Penfeld estuary, the castle was miraculously spared by the bombs of World War II and now stands as almost the only reminder of Brest's past. Built in the 12th century but later remodelled, it houses an extensive maritime museum.

and rises 26m (85ft) to allow ships in and out of the Penfeld estuary.

Tour Tanguy

Facing the castle is the city's only major relic of medieval times. Now the tower functions as the **Musée Municipal du Vieux Brest**, preserving the memory of pre- and post-Revolution Brest.
Opposite the castle on the River Penfeld. Tel: 02 98 00 88 60. Open: June–Sept daily 10am–noon & 2–7pm; Oct–May Tue & Thur 2–5pm; Sat & Sun 2–6pm. Free admission.

Brest is 70km (43 miles) northwest of Quimper on the fast N165 dual carriageway.

Brignogan-Plage

This popular seaside resort in north Finistère lies at the centre of the Côte des Légendes, known locally as Pagan Country, a surprising term considering the number of chapels and granite crosses strewn about the countryside.

The people of ancient Léon had the reputation of being less friendly than other Bretons; one legend even tells how at night they would tie lanterns to the horns of their cows to lure passing ships on to the reefs. Today, the coastal fringe forms part of the Ceinture Dorée (Golden Belt), and produces great quantities of onions, cauliflowers, artichokes and other vegetables.

Finistère

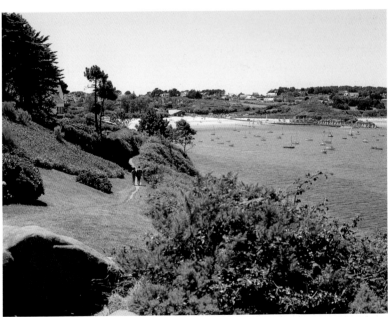

The view over a Carantec beach from the rocky platform known as La Chaise du Curé (Priest's Chair)

At Brignogan, sandy beaches alternate with large rock formations. On the way to the Pointe de Pontusval nearby, you can see an 8m (26ft) high menhir (standing stone), a base for a cross. Interesting cycle trips in the area include the ancient village of Goulven (7km/4 miles south) and Guissény resort (9km/6 miles southwest).

33km (21 miles) northeast of Brest on the D788 and D770.

Carantec

Carantec has all the ingredients which are necessary to make a family holiday a memorable success: sea, sand and scenery. Occupying a prominent position inside the Bay of Morlaix, its curve of sheltered beaches is interrupted to the northeast by picturesque cliffs facing the 16th-century Château du Taureau, and several small islands (now the protected nesting grounds of thousands of birds).

Gourmets will appreciate the fresh supply of oysters from the oyster beds south of Pointe de Pen-al-Lann near the Plage du Clouet.

To the northwest lies Île Callot, accessible on foot at low tide, with its sandy creeks as well as outcrops of granite.

15km (9 miles) northwest of Morlaix on the D73 and D173.

Carhaix-Plouguer

In Gallo-Roman Brittany, Carhaix-Plouguer was a thriving trading town and the capital of what is now Finistère.

Châteaulin: angling takes place downstream of the town, whose coat of arms features a salmon

The well-preserved bridge on the River Hyère, just north of the city, dates from that period. Today, it is an important dairy centre.

Like all self-respecting Breton towns and villages, Carhaix has its hero, and its legend. The hero is a modest Breton (an unusual combination), known as La Tour d'Auvergne, who repeatedly distinguished himself in Napoleon's army, but refused promotions and medals. He was made First Grenadier of the Republic by Bonaparte himself shortly before dying in action in 1800. His memory is honoured every year in June.

The legend is somewhat gruesome. Many centuries ago, there was a local Bluebeard who, fearful about being killed by a son, killed each wife as soon as she was pregnant. The fifth wife saved her child with the help of St Gildas, but eventually the Bluebeard discovered his child, and had him beheaded. Then along came St Trémeur, who picked up the head and carried it to the Bluebeard's castle. He threw a handful of sand at the castle, whereupon it crumbled to dust. A statue of St Trémeur with the boy's head stands over the fine Gothic portal of the Église St-Trémeur. Inside, there is a beautiful Renaissance altarpiece.

Nearby

There are two charming parish closes at **Cléden-Poher** and **St-Hernin**, with particularly fine calvaries.
9km (6 miles) southwest of Carhaix-Plouguer.

Carhaix-Plouguer is 70km (43 miles) northeast of Quimper on the D787.

Château de Kerjean

This splendid example of 16th-century architecture caused Louis XIII to proclaim it 'one of the handsomest houses in the kingdom'. Surrounded by double ramparts and a moat, the Renaissance-style castle influenced other constructions in the area, including the famous parish closes. Partly destroyed by fire in 1710, it was bought by the State in 1911 and restored, except for the right wing. It contains a remarkable collection of ancient Breton furniture. In the vast grounds, a park covering 20 hectares (49 acres), are a charming fountain and a superb dovecote.
10km (6 miles) north of Landivisiau. Tel: 02 98 69 93 69; www.chateau-de-kerjean.com. Open: Apr, May & Oct Wed–Mon 2–6pm; June & Sept Wed–Mon 1–6pm; July & Aug Wed–Mon 10am–7pm; Nov–Mar, Wed & Sun 2–5pm. Closed: Tue. Admission charge.

Châteaulin

This sleepy riverside town, on the edge of the Parc Naturel Régional d'Armorique, is a famous salmon-fishing centre. Traditional granite houses, neatly lining the embankments, are reflected in the still waters of the canalised River Aulne.

A parish close stands among the ruins of the castle, overlooking the river and the town. An arched gateway leads to the **Église Notre-Dame** (once the chapel of Châteaulin castle), recently restored and graced by a slender Renaissance tower. The calvary dates from the 15th century and the ossuary, adjacent to the church, from the 16th century (access from the rue Graveran).

Chapelle St-Côme

Beautifully proportioned, this rural chapel boasts elegant carvings of floral and animal motifs along the cornice at the base of the vaulting.
19km (12 miles) west of Châteaulin on the D887, then the D108 and the D63.

Ménez-Hom

From its isolated position, the 330m (1,083ft) high mountain peak offers exceptional views of the Baie de Douarnenez, the Crozon Peninsula, Cap Sizun and, closer, the Aulne estuary and the Pont de Térénez.

15km (9 miles) west of Châteaulin on the D887, then right on the D83.

Châteaulin is 30km (19 miles) north of Quimper on the N165 dual carriageway.

Concarneau

One of France's most important fishing ports, Concarneau specialises in tuna caught off the coast of Africa and processed in three local canneries. Its delightful harbour has been guarded since the 14th century by the famous Ville Close (Walled City). Built on a small island barring the entrance to the harbour, the Ville Close is completely surrounded by defensive walls and towers. From the top of the walls, a fine view extends over the fishing port with

In the parish close of Daoulas, three sides of the elegant 12th-century cloister still stand

its vast *criée* (auction hall) and the marina on the other side.

Boat trips are available to the Glénan island of St-Nicolas (1 hour 10 minutes) and to Beg-Meil across the Baie de la Forêt (30 minutes). The Pointe du Cabellou, facing the entrance to the harbour, is a good place for a scenic cycling tour.

Musée de la Pêche

This comprehensive museum – part inside, part outside the old walls – covers all activities associated with fishing, including shipbuilding, canning and sea rescue.

Rue Vauban. Tel: 02 98 97 10 20; www.concarneau.org. Open: daily July & Aug 9.30am–8pm; Apr–June 10am–6pm; Sept–Mar 10am–noon & 2–6pm. Admission charge.

Concarneau is 21km (13 miles) southeast of Quimper on the D783.

Crozon Peninsula

See pp110–11.

Daoulas

Now a cultural centre, the village is famous for its abbey, which was founded in the 6th century and rebuilt 600 years later. The abbey prospered until the Revolution. The buildings we see today are from different periods. A 16th-century porch marks the entrance to the parish close. The former abbey church has kept its Romanesque west front and imposing nave. The cloister,

unique in Brittany, has 32 Romanesque arches, varied ornamentation and, in the centre, a stone basin decorated with curious grotesques. In the grounds are a medicinal plant garden, a 16th-century fountain and a small oratory.
Tel: 02 98 25 84 39; www.abbaye-daoulas.com. Open: Apr–Dec daily 10.30am–6.30pm. Admission charge.

Daoulas is 20km (12 miles) southeast of Brest on the N165.

Douarnenez

Sardine-fishing brought prosperity to this historic fishing port in the mid-19th century, when canneries employed a great number of women. Next came lobster-fishing along the coast of Africa. Now Douarnenez divides its efforts between local and long-distance fishing

THE DROWNED CITY OF YS

Some 1,400 years ago, King Gradlon lived in the beautiful city of Ys, on the shores of Douarnenez Bay. His daughter led such a dissolute life that God sent a handsome stranger to punish her. The stranger tricked her into giving him the keys that opened the dikes protecting the city from the sea, and the waters flooded into the city. Woken by St Guénolé, the king jumped on his horse with his daughter, but St Guénolé ordered him to let go of her, and she met a watery end. In good weather, fishermen still claim to hear the bells of Ys ringing beneath the sea.

to keep its high rank among the fishing ports of France. Visit the harbour at night, when the day's catch is being unloaded.

There is superb scenery round the bay here, which enclosed the legendary city of Ys, submerged by the sea (*see*

Full of character, the church at Le Faou is set beside the river after which the town is named box). The bay is a watersports centre, with sailing schools, surfing and beaches a few kilometres away. Part of the old harbour has recently been turned into a museum, unique in Europe. From the marina at the entrance of Port-Rhu, a path follows the coast past Tristan Island (where the famous lovers Tristan and Isolde are said to have taken refuge), skirts the Plage des Sables Blancs and leads to the Pointe de Leydé, which offers panoramic views of Douarnenez Bay.

Port-Musée

Housed in a former cannery, the museum is devoted to traditional boats of all kinds and sizes from all over Europe. In the fascinating open-air section along the quayside of Port-Rhu, the floating part of the museum re-creates the colourful harbour animation of the past. At present, only three of the boats can be visited.

The 16th-century Pont de Rohan, in Landerneau, is one of the last inhabited bridges in Europe

Place de l'Enfer. Tel: 02 98 92 65 20; www.port-musee.org. Open: mid-June–mid-Sept daily 10am–7pm; mid-Apr–mid-June & mid-Sept–early Nov Tue–Sun 10am–12.30pm & 2–6pm. Closed: Mon off-season. Admission charge.

Douarnenez is 23km (14 miles) northwest of Quimper on the D765.

Le Faou

Gabled houses with slate-covered façades, dating from the 16th century, line one side of the high street of this charming old village. The church has a richly carved south porch. Le Faou is a good starting point for excursions to the Crozon Peninsula and the Monts d'Arrée.

Landévennec Abbey

The ruins of the Benedictine abbey, founded in the 5th century by the Welsh monk Gwennolé, have a lovely rural setting at the entrance of the Aulne estuary. The church is said to contain the grave of King Gradlon (*see box, p93*). A museum illustrates the abbey's history.
21km (13 miles) west of Le Faou on the D791 and D60. Tel: 02 98 27 35 90. Open: Apr–June Sun–Fri 2–6pm; July–Sept daily 10am–7pm. Admission charge.

Le Faou is 32km (20 miles) southeast of Brest off the N165.

Le Folgoët

Famous for its splendid basilica and its *pardon* in September – one of the most important in Brittany – this modest village and pilgrimage centre owes its name to yet another legend. Folgoët means 'Madman's Wood', and the madman in question was a poor simpleton who lived near a spring on the edge of the forest and could say only two words: Ave Maria. When he died, a white lily grew on his grave bearing those very words in gold letters. A church dedicated to Our Lady was built over the spring. The building was completed in 1423.

Notre-Dame Basilica

The most striking feature of this massive Gothic basilica is undoubtedly the granite rood screen, admirably proportioned and delicately carved. At the east end of the building, a fountain is fed by the spring running beneath the altar.

Le Folgoët is 23km (14 miles) northeast of Brest on the D788.

Fouesnant

This very pleasant little town, set among fruit orchards on the Baie de la Forêt, produces the best cider in Brittany, according to the locals. In its sheltered position on the west side of the bay, Fouesnant is dotted with wooded sand dunes. During the Fête des Pommiers (Apple Tree Festival), in July, you can see women wearing their exquisite lace headdresses, each one unique to its district with its own particular shape.

La Forêt-Fouesnant

This idyllic village, at the end of a deep bay, is a popular sailing and walking area. Its charming parish close has an interesting 16th-century calvary, and the typically Breton church has a granite steeple.
3.5km (2 miles) northeast of Fouesnant.

Fouesnant is 15km (9 miles) southeast of Quimper on the D45 and D34.

Guerlesquin

See p147.

Huelgoat

See p142.

Landerneau

Landerneau is one of those estuary towns that prospered from the 16th century through a thriving export trade with Spain and Portugal. The picturesque bridge spanning the River Elorn was built by the Rohan family, who once owned the town.

The town is now the commercial centre of a rich agricultural area. On the place St-Thomas on the left bank is the Église St-Thomas-de-Cantorbéry, with its curious three-tiered steeple. A small Renaissance ossuary stands nearby.
20km (12 miles) northeast of Brest on the D712.

Locronan

This gem of a village presents a remarkable ensemble of Renaissance domestic architecture, the heritage of its prosperous days as a centre of sailcloth manufacture. Time seems not to have touched medieval Locronan, and dedicated craftsmen keep alive the skills of woodcarving, glass-blowing and weaving in wool, linen and silk.

The imposing church dominating the main square is dedicated to St Ronan, an Irish hermit who lived in a nearby forest and used to climb barefoot up a nearby hill, the Montagne de Locronan. During the July *pardon* (called a *troménie* here), the procession of pilgrims follows in the saint's footsteps.

Ste-Anne-la-Palud

The 19th-century chapel of Ste-Anne stands among sand dunes on the shores of Douarnenez Bay. Every year at the end of August, the area is invaded by a colourful crowd attending one of the most famous *pardons* in Brittany.
8km (5 miles) northwest of Locronan on the D63.

Locronan is 10km (6 miles) east of Douarnenez on the D7.

Monts d'Arrée

See Parc Naturel Régional d'Armorique, *p143.*

Montagnes Noires

Together with the Monts d'Arrée in the north, the Black Mountains form the

Shopping or just strolling is a pleasure to be savoured in the streets of old Morlaix

east–west backbone of Brittany. Written across a map, 'Montagnes Noires' may seem a pompous designation since the highest summit is only 326m (1,070ft), but the expansive vistas, the outcrops of sombre rock and a dark mantle of forest justify the term – with a little imagination, of course!

The small towns of Gourin and Châteauneuf-du-Faou are good starting points for a sightseeing trip. Gourin was once a thriving town, the centre of slate extraction, but part of its population emigrated to America during the 19th century. A few kilometres northwest on the D301, you can climb the highest peak, the Roc de Toullaëron, from where the view extends far and wide.

The idyllic setting of Châteauneuf-du-Faou appealed to Paul Sérusier, one of Gauguin's friends who decorated one of the chapels in the church. For amateur anglers the location overlooking the River Aulne is a paradise. South of the river lies the **Domaine de Trévarez**, combining outdoor and cultural entertainment (*see p143*).

Morlaix

Morlaix occupies the bottom of a deep, almost canyon-like valley, spanned by a huge viaduct casting its shadow on the town. The long estuary, known as the Rivière de Morlaix, provided a means for the export of linen cloth famed all over Europe, which ensured Morlaix's prosperity for nearly 500 years. The harbour expanded downriver, where rich shipowners built stately homes along the quayside. In the 18th century, Morlaix was almost as famous for privateering in merchant shipping as St-Malo. Today, the harbour shelters a more peaceful flotilla of yachts.

The medieval town lies at the foot of the viaduct, which carries the main Paris–Brest railway line. Along the pedestrianised Grand Rue and the narrow streets known as *venelles*, there are still many timber-framed corbelled houses, built between the 15th and the 17th centuries. The most famous is the Maison de la Reine Anne in the rue du Mur, decorated with statues of saints and grotesques.

Not far away is the **Église St-Mathieu**, rebuilt in 1824 and worth a visit for its medieval statue of the Virgin and Child, which opens up like a triptych.

Musée des Jacobins

Housed in a former church, the museum contains archaeological finds, a fine collection of Breton furniture and some interesting religious statues. *Place des Jacobins. Tel: 02 98 88 68 88; www.musee.ville.morlaix.fr. Open: July & Aug daily 10am–12.30pm & 2–6.30pm; Apr, May & Sept Wed–Mon 10am–noon & 2–6pm; June & Oct–Mar Mon & Wed–Sat 10am–noon & 2–5pm. Closed: Tue, Sun off-season. Admission charge.*

Morlaix is 60km (37 miles) northeast of Brest on the N12 dual carriageway.

Île d'Ouessant

Separated from the mainland by one of the strongest tidal currents in the world and often surrounded by a veil of mist, Ouessant is a holiday centre known for its rugged terrain: the once cultivated land is now virtually treeless.

But the island seems to have found a promising new source of income – the (*cont on p100*)

Morlaix's viaduct, with its elongated arches, crosses the River Dossen at a towering height

Calvaries and parish closes

Porch ornamentation, Guimiliau

The Christianising of Druidic standing stones, surmounting them with crucifixes or carving Christian symbols on them, was an early sign of the religious evolution of the Bretons, a deeply spiritual people. This evolution gained momentum over the centuries to culminate in an explosion of artistic creation, whose greatest expression was the parish close. These unique architectural entities flourished in Brittany – and more specifically in and around the Elorn Valley – with the flowering of the Renaissance, between the 15th and the 17th centuries. They recall a time when everyday life centred around the parish.

A message in stone

Situated at the heart of the village, the close is entered through a monumental gate usually leading straight into the cemetery and symbolising access to eternal life. The church stands at the centre, small but profusely ornamented both outside and inside, with elaborate christening fonts and pulpits, luminous rood beams and beautiful altarpieces. Ossuaries, originally leaning against the church, gradually assumed the new role of funeral chapels and became separate buildings. Near the church, and often in front of it, stands the calvary, a direct descendant of those simple crosses erected by the wayside, in fields or facing the sea. The elaborate calvaries, known all over the world as a distinctive feature of Breton religious art, are often remarkably complex; designed to instruct a largely illiterate population, they are like a three-dimensional Bible with as many as 200 characters displayed round a solid granite base.

An invitation to meditate

Like the great medieval cathedrals, these grey stone parish closes combine the spiritual and the aesthetic in a way that defies indifference. For the strong beliefs of a people are there in front of our eyes, carved in local granite: their conviction that eternal life can be touched through a beautiful work of art, their blend of realism with an inclination towards the supernatural, their love of powerful symbols. But there is more: parish closes express a belief in social order and in the need to perpetuate that order through teaching. They also suggest the desire of a community to assert its religious identity for all posterity.

Guéhenno's calvary

farming of seaweed. As part of the Parc Naturel Régional d'Armorique, Ouessant also promotes a new kind of tourism, emphasising the discovery of nature and the rediscovery of old traditions.

Ecomusée

Two traditional houses, containing furniture, costumes and tools, illustrate daily life on Ouessant in the past. *Niou Huella. Tel: 02 98 48 86 37; www. ot-ouessant.fr. Open: Apr–Sept daily 10.30am–6.30pm; Jan–Mar & Oct–Dec Tue–Sun 1.30–5pm. Closed: Mon off-season. Admission charge.*

Musée des Phares et Balises

Appropriately located in a lighthouse, the museum is devoted to the history of lighthouses and their keepers since ancient times.

Parish closes

Phare du Créac'h. Tel: 02 98 48 80 70; www.ouessant.fr. Open: as for Ecomusée. Admission charge.

Access by boat from le Conquet (1 hour), by air from Brest (15 minutes).

Parish closes

The concentration of parish closes in a relatively small area lends itself to a convenient day trip, starting from Landerneau or from Landivisiau.

Guimiliau

The striking calvary offers a complex yet harmonious arrangement of 200 characters over an arched base, depicting scenes from the life of Jesus and from his Passion. The church interior is also remarkable and includes a christening font beneath a baldachin, a finely carved pulpit and a 17th-century organ.

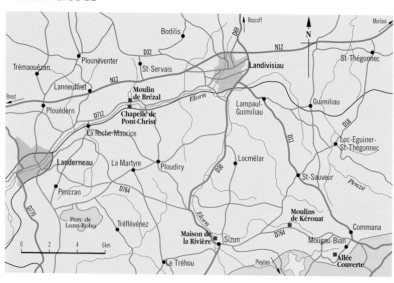

7.5km (5 miles) southeast of Landivisiau on the D11.

Lampaul-Guimiliau

Here the artists concentrated on the church. A feast of colours welcomes you inside: the rood beam decorated with a frieze in a lively naïve style, the magnificent retable in high relief, the elegant baptistery and a beautiful *pietà* carved from a single piece of wood.
4km (2¹/₂ miles) southeast of Landivisiau on the D11.

La Martyre

This small village has the oldest parish close in the area, with the calvary set on top of the gate. Note the lovely south porch of the church and the extensive interior decoration.
6km (4 miles) east of Landerneau.

La Roche-Maurice

The church contains a rare Renaissance rood screen and a 16th-century stained-glass window throwing light on the main altar. Above the holy water basin outside the ossuary, Death threatens a group of people with an arrow, saying '*Je vous tue tous*' (I kill you all).
4.5km (3 miles) northeast of Landerneau on the D712.

St-Thégonnec

For two centuries, there was intense rivalry between St-Thégonnec and Guimiliau nearby, each town trying to surpass the other in splendour.

The River Aven once powered many mills, but is now at the service of Pont-Aven's boat users

The result is a remarkable church and an ossuary chapel. Note particularly the domed Renaissance tower of the church and, inside, the carved pulpit that dates from 1683.
9km (6 miles) east of Landivisiau on the N12 dual carriageway.

Sizun

With its triple arch and Corinthian columns, the monumental gate is reminiscent of Roman ceremonial arches. Note also the 16th-century ossuary chapel, with its small museum.
12km (7 miles) southeast of Landerneau on the D764.

There is another famous parish close further south in Pleyben, northeast of Châteaulin (*see p91*). The calvary has a truly monumental base, although the whole is not so harmonious as in Guimiliau.

Plougastel-Daoulas

This small town is the commercial centre of the Plougastel Peninsula,
(*cont on p104*)

Gauguin and the School of Pont-Aven

When Gauguin arrived in Pont-Aven in 1886, he had already begun to move away from Impressionism. Looking for new forms of expression, he hoped to find in Brittany a simpler and more authentic way of life that would enable him to return to the roots of Art.

At Pont-Aven he met another painter, Émile Bernard, in the boarding house run by Marie-Jeanne Gloanec where, for the next ten years, many artists would stay and work. In 1888 Paul Sérusier arrived in the town and the three of them became the exponents of a new style of painting, Synthétisme, in which the artist's vision took precedence over reality (their motto was 'Paint what you see, not what is there'). Experimental techniques found favour: the use of strongly contrasting colours and a return to the principles of drawing by underlining the contours of objects and figures.

Other artists joined the first three: Charles Laval, Henri Maufra, Émile Schuffenecker, Meyer de Haan and many others. Soon there were some 20 of them staying at the Gloanec boarding house.

In 1889 Gauguin painted the famous *Le Christ Jaune* (*The Yellow Christ*) against an idyllic rural background, and *La Lutte de Jacob et de l'Ange* (*Jacob Fighting the Angel*), which shows that he was all the time striving for greater simplicity and becoming more daring in his compositions.

Retreat to Le Pouldu
When tourists began flocking to Pont-Aven and Gauguin felt that the place

Pont-Aven, a haven for artists

Gauguin, self-portrait in Breton costume

was losing its original charm, he decided to move to Le Pouldu, a seaside village further south. With Laval, Filiger and Meyer de Haan, he settled in Marie Henry's inn (*see p104*).

Gauguin's influence continued to grow, his personality dominating the other painters who, in spite of being split into two groups, became known as the School of Pont-Aven. It was not, of course, a school in the literal sense: they were simply a group of artists working and searching together for new means to transcend reality. In their search, these men became the forefathers of modern painting and of such movements as Expressionism, Surrealism and even Abstract art.

famous for its strawberries and early vegetables.

The calvary, built between 1602 and 1604 after an epidemic of plague had devastated the area, ranks among the finest in Brittany. It suffered bomb damage in 1944, but was restored thanks to the generosity of an American officer.
10km (6 miles) southeast of Brest on the N165.

Pont-Aven

This small river port prospered as a mill town and acquired international fame when a group of artists – later known as the School of Pont-Aven – gathered there round Paul Gauguin (*see pp102–3*). Delightful riverside walks around the town take you along the Promenade Xavier Grall up to the Bois d'Amour, and in the other direction towards the harbour; they include marked paths that identify the locations of famous paintings. On the outskirts of town stands the Chapelle de Trémalo. Its crucified Christ served as the model for Gauguin's famous *Le Christ Jaune* (*The Yellow Christ*).

Musée

Apart from its permanent collection of works by the Pont-Aven group (none by Gauguin himself), the museum illustrates life in the town in Gauguin's time with the help of old photographs.
Place de l'Hôtel de Ville. Tel: 02 98 06 14 43; www.pontaven.com. Open: daily July & Aug 10am–7pm; Sept–Dec & Feb–June 10am–12.30pm & 2–6pm.

Admission charge.
Pont-Aven is 14km (9 miles) southeast of Concarneau on the D783.

Pont-l'Abbé
See p112.

Le Pouldu

Facing south, the sheltered Plage des Grands Sables is backed by high cliffs; steps climb up to a promenade lined with hotels. Nearby is a monument to Paul Gauguin, who spent a great deal of time in Le Pouldu between 1889 and 1894. He lived with his friends in the house of Marie Henry, which they decorated profusely. The unique interior has been faithfully reconstructed in an identical house a few metres away, which also houses temporary exhibitions related to Gauguin and his friends.

The harbour is picturesquely situated at the mouth of the River Laïta, 2km ($1^1/4$ miles) away. The town is a popular horse-riding centre.
Maison Marie Henry, 10 rue des Grands Sables. Tel: 02 98 39 98 51. Open: July & Aug daily; Apr–June & Sept–mid-Nov Thur–Sun (Wed–Sun in June & Sept). Guided tours only; call for times. Admission charge.

13km (8 miles) south of Quimperlé on the D49.

Primel-Trégastel

This resort is situated on the green hills of a narrow peninsula in a setting similar to the Côte de Granit Rose.

A quiet street in Quimperlé's upper town

The sandy beach stretches over 1km (²/₃ mile) towards the Pointe de Primel and its striking pink rock formations. The view extends across the Bay of Morlaix to the lighthouse on the Île de Batz.

Le Diben

This charming fishing port specialises in shellfish stored in large seawater pools (visitors welcome). Walk to the Pointe de Diben for more enchanting views of the Bay of Morlaix.
2.5km (1¹/₂ miles) west of Primel-Trégastel on the D46a.

St-Jean-du-Doigt

The village gets its curious name from a relic: the finger of St John the Baptist, supposedly brought back from the Holy Land in the 15th century. Pilgrims soon flocked to St-Jean-du-Doigt, as the relic was said to cure eye diseases. Nowadays, a *pardon* takes place in June. The parish close includes a monumental gate, a high Renaissance fountain and an oratory.
6km (4 miles) southeast of Primel-Trégastel on the D46 and D79.

Cairn de Barnenez

Following the scenic coast road south to Morlaix, a right turn at St-Gonven takes you out on the Kernéhélen Peninsula. There you can see two rough stone structures overlooking the Bay of Morlaix, containing 11 passage graves from around 4600 BC.
12km (7 miles) south of Primel-Trégastel off the D76. Tel: 02 98 67 24 73; www.monum.fr. Open: May–Aug daily 10am–6.30pm; Sept–Apr Tue–Sun 10am–12.30pm & 2–5.30pm. Closed: Mon off-season. Admission charge.

Primel-Trégastel is 25km (16 miles) north of Morlaix.

Quimperlé

This beautiful old town developed on an island at the confluence of the Ellé and Isole rivers. As it grew it climbed on to the plateau; the new district was called the Ville Haute (High Town), while the medieval town became known as the Ville Basse (Low Town). The Ville Basse has retained part of its medieval character around its magnificent church. Along the rue Brémond-d'Ars are several stately stone-built houses dating from the 17th century, and nearby are the ruins of the Église St-Colomban.

Église Ste-Croix

Built at the end of the 11th century and based on Jerusalem's Church of the Holy Sepulchre, Ste-Croix was heavily restored in the 19th century; however, the crypt and the apse are original. Note the beautifully carved capitals atop the short columns of the crypt. *Rue de la Paix.*

The fine view from St-Pol-de-Léon's Kreisker chapel tower takes in the former cathedral

Maison des Archers

This is the best of several late medieval houses lining a narrow cobbled street. It houses a local museum devoted to the town and costumes of the region. *7 rue Dom-Morice. Tel: 02 98 96 04 32. Open: July & Aug 10am–noon & 2–7pm. Closed: Sun morning & Mon. Admission charge.*

La Roche du Diable

From the top of the 'Devil's Rock' there is an impressive view over the River Ellé. *12km (7 miles) northeast of Quimperlé on the D790 and a road to the right.*

Quimperlé is 47km (29 miles) southeast of Quimper on the N165 dual carriageway.

Roscoff

Once the hideout of notorious privateers, Roscoff is today known for the mildness of its climate, fine beaches and sophisticated hydrotherapy centres. It also has an important fishing fleet specialising in shellfish, and the unloading of the lobster trawlers in the old harbour is always a fascinating sight. The tiny Chapelle Ste-Barbe, built on an outcrop at the Pointe de Bloscon, overlooks the seawater pools where lobsters and crabs are stocked. Beyond lies the port of Roscoff, from which Brittany Ferries sail to Plymouth and Cork. West of the fishing harbour and marina is the rue Amiral-Réveillère, with fine 16th-century stone houses.

An abundance of flowers welcomes visitors to the offshore island of Île de Batz (15 minutes by ferry from the port). The island is surrounded by dunes and sandy beaches, and seaweed-gathering is one of the rare traditional occupations to have survived, although today the heavy cartloads are pulled by tractors rather than horses. The island's *école de mer* offers sea canoeing and orthodox sailing. The top of the lighthouse on the west side offers a good overall view.

Aquarium

Part of the Musée Océanologique is devoted to local marine flora and fauna presented in several pools that re-create their natural environment. The Aquarium is currently closed for renovation.

Place G Tessier. Tel: 02 98 29 23 25. Open: daily 10am–noon & 1–6pm. Admission charge.

Église Notre-Dame-de-Kroaz-Batz

This 16th-century church has a very distinctive Renaissance steeple decorated with amusing lanterns delicately carved in granite. Carvings of ships and guns on the walls are reminders of the town's privateering past. Note the 15th-century alabaster retable in the right-hand aisle.

Place Lacaze-Duthiers.

Roscoff is 25km (16 miles) northwest of Morlaix on the D58.

St-Pol-de-Léon

The soaring steeple of the Chapelle du Kreisker belongs to the highest belfry in Brittany and is a striking example of

Fascinating modern sculpture at the museum of Pointe du Raz near Cap Sizun

refined Gothic tracery. It certainly provides a very good reason to visit this compact, ancient town, one of the seven original Breton bishoprics, with its fine Norman-style cathedral containing a 10th-century sarcophagus and the relics of its founder.

Nearby

The 15th-century feudal **Château de Kérouzéré** has retained only three of its machicolated corner towers. The castle contains tapestries and Breton furniture, and the oratory is decorated with 17th-century frescoes.

8km (5 miles) west of St-Pol off the D10.

St-Pol-de-Léon is 20km (12 miles) northwest of Morlaix on the D58.

Cap Sizun

Cap Sizun's jagged promontory offers a bitter contest between land and sea. Between the Pointe du Raz and the Île de Sein lies the Raz de Sein, the subject of shipwreck stories. A path follows the edge of the cliff to the Enfer de Plogoff, a precipice where locals claim to hear the cries of damned souls.

Across the Baie des Trépassés, the **Pointe du Van** offers great views. Along the north coast, the **Réserve du Cap Sizun** is a bird sanctuary.

Réserve du Cap Sizun, Goulien. Tel: 02 98 70 13 53. Open: daily July & Aug 10am–6pm; Apr–June 10am–noon & 2–6pm. Closed: Sept–Mar. Admission charge.

50km (31 miles) northwest of Quimper.

Walk: Old Quimper

The oldest and most charming district of Quimper lies north of the River Odet in the vicinity of Cathédrale St-Corentin. A relaxing stroll through narrow cobbled streets will enable you to admire a fascinating variety of domestic architecture, beautifully restored timber-framed and stone houses with a wealth of interesting and often amusing carvings.

Allow 1½ hours.

Start in front of the Hôtel de Ville on the north side of the cathedral; note the strength and elegance of the flying buttresses and the elaborate porch. Follow the rue du Frout and turn right to reach the River Odet; turn right again.

1 The town walls

With the river on the left and a well-preserved section of the medieval town walls on the right, this part of the embankment is particularly attractive. The spires of the cathedral can be seen towering above the walls, in contrast to the red geraniums decorating the many footbridges spanning the Odet.

The rue du Roi Gradlon on the right leads past the Musée Départemental Breton to the place St-Corentin. Walk across the square.

2 Place St-Corentin

On your right stands the imposing cathedral, while on your left a splendid 15th-century house has been turned into a shop called L'Art de Cornouaille, which sells specialities from the region including the famous Quimper ceramics.

Follow the rue Elie Fréron up to No 22, faced with slates. Turn back and bear right when you reach the tiny place au Beurre, where you can stop for a snack at one of the crêperies.

3 Rues du Sallé and du Guéodet

All the streets in this area are worth exploring as they contribute a great deal to the unique atmosphere of old Quimper. No 10 rue du Sallé is particularly fine, but it is the Maison des Cariatides in the rue du Guéodet that attracts most attention, so vivid are the expressions on the faces carved below the corbel.

Turn right to return to the square and right again into the rue Kéréon.

4 Rue Kéréon

This is the high street of the old town, lined with timber-framed corbelled

houses and elegant boutiques. The graceful outline of the cathedral appears at one end of the street, while at the other end a delightful view awaits you. A small bridge, formerly a drawbridge, spans the River Steir, and on the left can be seen part of the old town wall and a picturesque *bartizan* (a projecting lookout).
Cross the bridge and turn left.

5 Place Terre-au-Duc

This was the centre of the medieval market town and is still surrounded with half-timbered houses. Nearby, the new covered market, erected in place of the old one, which burned down in 1979, blends very tastefully with the old houses close to it. Walk along the quai du Port au Vin and quai du Steir, whose names may seem strange to you since

there is no river in sight – but in fact, the Steir has been canalised and covered over at that point.
Turn left when you reach the embankment.

6 Rue du Parc

The wide pavement along the embankment is constantly crowded with strollers, shoppers and business people, everyone walking along at their own pace among the tables and chairs laid out in front of the attractive restaurants and cafés.

At the corner of the rue St-François, an old-fashioned shop, called Faïences de Quimper, displays colourful specimens of the famous local ceramics. *A little further on the left, the rue du Roi Gradlon takes you back to the place St-Corentin and the Hôtel de Ville.*

By bike: The Crozon Peninsula

These two cycle tours take in the scenic countryside at the extremity of the Crozon Peninsula, an area of wild beauty now included in the Parc Naturel Régional d'Armorique.

Tour 1 takes about half a day and explores the northern part of Crozon around Camaret-sur-Mer.

Although less spectacular, tour 2 of the southern Crozon Peninsula gives a good overall impression of this heath-covered area (allow half a day).

TOUR 1 (the orange route)
1 Camaret-sur-Mer

This lively seaside resort and fishing port occupies a sheltered position inside a cove formed by the Sillon de Camaret. The fort built by Vauban at the tip of this sandbank is a reminder that Camaret once guarded the entrance to Brest harbour.
Follow the D55 east to St-Fiacre, turn left on the D355, and continue along the road that closely follows the coast to the Pointe des Espagnols.

2 Pointe des Espagnols

Overlooking the entrance of Brest harbour, the point gets its name from a fort built there by Spanish troops to blockade Brest in support of the Catholic cause during the 16th-century Wars of Religion. The fort was later razed to the ground. The view extends over Brest, the Elorn estuary and the Plougastel Peninsula.
The road skirts the strait known as the Goulet de Brest, then turns south towards
Camaret. Continue west to the Pointe du Toulinguet. Turn back, then first right; your next stop is the Pointe de Pen-Hir.

3 Pointe de Pen-Hir

Just outside Camaret you will pass a group of megaliths (*see pp124–5*) known as the **Alignements de Lagatjar**. These consist of three rows of standing stones – over 140 in all – most of which had fallen and were raised again in the 1930s. Seen from the top of the 70m (230ft) high cliff there is a sheer drop to dark jagged rocks and the famous **Tas de Pois**, pyramid-shaped reefs. A monument honours the Free French forces of World War II.
Return to Camaret.

TOUR 2 (the green route)
Start from the resort of Crozon; follow the D308 west to the Pointe de Dinan.

1 Pointe de Dinan

The attraction here is the **Château de Dinan**, a huge rock looking like a castle, linked to the main part of the cliff by a natural arch; this gives access for those who wish to explore further. *Turn back, then head south towards Cap de la Chèvre. The Plage de la Palud on the right is dangerous, but it offers close-up views of the rocky coastline.*

2 Cap de la Chèvre

Views extend over the whole length of Cap Sizun prolonged by the Île de Sein. A former German observation post stands at the furthest point.
Turn back.

3 St-Hernot

Housed in the old village school, the **Maison des Minéraux** exhibits over 500 minerals from all over Brittany.
Continue to Morgat on the D887.

4 Morgat

Morgat has a kind of old-world charm. Its sheltered beach draws many families, while the plentiful local fishing grounds are popular with fishing enthusiasts. Several interesting caves can be visited by boat from the harbour.
Return to Crozon.

By bike: The Crozon Peninsula

Tour: In the painters' footsteps

During the 19th century, several groups of painters 'discovered' Brittany. Quite a few of these artists were seduced by the remote region of Cornouaille, its unspoilt landscapes, its unaffected people and the harmony between man and nature. This 100-km (62-mile) long tour takes you through Bigouden country.

Allow a whole day.

Start the tour from Quimper, where the Musée des Beaux-Arts has a fine collection of 19th- and 20th-century paintings of Breton inspiration that are worth viewing. Drive south on the D34 to Bénodet, then cross the River Odet.

1 Ste-Marine

Facing Bénodet across the river, the village centre forms a charming setting with its church and tiny harbour.
Drive back to the main road, turn left, then left again on the D144.

2 Île-Tudy

In spite of its name, Île-Tudy is no longer an island. Facing Loctudy across a narrow strait, it is an attractive traditional seaside village.
Return to the main road and turn left.

3 Pont-l'Abbé

The castle keep houses the Musée Bigouden containing furniture, handicrafts and costumes. On the way to Loctudy, 2km (1¼ miles) out of town, the Maison du Pays Bigouden is a farm illustrating daily life at the end of the 19th century.
Musée Bigouden. Tel: 02 98 66 09 03. Open: daily June–Sept 10am–12.30pm & 2–6.30pm; mid-Apr–May 2–6pm. Closed: Oct–mid-Apr. Admission charge. Maison du Pays Bigouden. Tel: 02 98 87 35 63. Open: June–Sept 2–6pm. Closed: Mon. Admission charge.
Continue on the D2.

4 Manoir de Kérazan

The original interior of this elegant manor house enhances a fine collection of paintings.
Tel: 02 98 87 40 40. Open: mid-June–Aug 10.30am–7pm; Apr–mid-June & Sept 2–6pm. Closed: Mon (except in summer). Admission charge.

5 Loctudy

This peaceful family resort is one of the busiest fishing ports on the south coast,

with a splendid church.
Drive west and turn left on the D102.

6 Lesconil

Lined with restaurants and typical
Breton houses, the fishing harbour
is particularly charming, livening
up between 5pm and 6pm when
the *malamoks* (small trawlers)
return.
Continue west along the coast.

7 Le Guilvinec

The fourth most important fishing
port in France, Le Guilvinec
specialises in some 60 different
varieties of fish.
Continue to Penmarc'h.

8 Penmarc'h and St-Guénolé

The area around Penmarc'h inspired
several generations of painters
including Lemordant. Look at the
Église St-Nonna, Penmarc'h, before
moving on to the Pointe de Penmarc'h.
Slightly north, St-Guénolé is famous for
its rocky shoreline.
Drive north along the coast.

9 Notre-Dame de Tronoën Calvary

Set among sand dunes close to the sea,
this is one of the oldest of Brittany's
great calvaries, dating from the mid-
15th century. An important *pardon*
takes place here in September.
Return to Quimper on the D156.

Tour: In the painters' footsteps

Southern Brittany

Although here the battle between land and sea is a thing of the past, it has nevertheless left its mark. The coastal area is indented by deep, wide estuaries and the vast expanse of the Golfe du Morbihan (now offering the safest bathing and sailing facilities in Brittany), while the fascinating marshland of the Grande Brière and the salt marshes of the Guérande Peninsula near La Baule were created by sand deposits.

One might be tempted to say that in southern Brittany everything happens along the coast, just as northern Brittany's life is organised round its busy Channel ports and resorts. Although not an entirely accurate description, it is true to say that southern Brittany's pulse is powered by its sunny shoreline.

Brittany's 'gentle' coastline

The word 'gentle' used to describe part of Brittany's coast might seem exaggerated. Yet, compared to the spectacular cliffs of the Côte d'Emeraude or the austere west coast round Cap Sizun and the Crozon Peninsula, the south coast appears definitely smoother and tamer – allowing for a few exceptions like the Côte Sauvage of the Quiberon Peninsula.

'Gentle' also because of its particularly mild and sunny climate, the south coast attracts crowds of holidaymakers to its fashionable beaches at Quiberon and La Baule ('the Nice of the North'). But there are also idyllic beaches all along the coast,

so those who prefer a more peaceful environment will find a wide choice, in particular between the Rhuys Peninsula and the Pointe du Croisic west of La Baule.

Another aspect of the area's attractions are its islands, many of which can be reached by scheduled boat trips. Île de Groix and above all Belle-Île, the largest island off the coast of Brittany, are well worth a visit.

Rivers and old towns

Several rivers – such as the Erdre, the Vilaine, the Blavet and their tributaries – wind their way towards the south coast through countryside and tracts of forest like the Landes de Lanvaux.

The Nantes–Brest Canal, running from east to west, links the Erdre, the Vilaine, the Oust and the Blavet, completing a network of waterways that appeals to river-cruising enthusiasts.

South of the canal, many towns retain their ancient character and a wealth of varied, well-preserved domestic architecture. Among them is Vannes, the capital of Morbihan; the walled town of Guérande; Rochefort-en-Terre, famous for its stone houses; and the riverside towns of Malestroit, Pontivy and Auray.

Southern Brittany also has some impressive examples of military architecture, including the splendid feudal castle at Josselin and the dramatic ruins of the Château de Suscinio, former residence of the dukes of Brittany, overlooking the sea.

Heritage of mystery and beauty

Just as Finistère is famous for its calvaries and parish closes, southern Brittany is famous for its megaliths, and in particular the *alignements* at Carnac.

Much has been written about these long rows of granite standing stones, but after several thousand years they remain mysterious (*see pp124–5*). However, massive and rude of shape, they in no way overshadow the refined beauty found elsewhere in the region in such artistic treasures as St-Fiacre Chapel, near Le Faouët to the west.

Southern Brittany

Nantes

Officially the capital of the Loire region but Breton at heart, Nantes lies at the confluence of the Loire and the Erdre, rivers that are now mostly canalised. The city followed the ups and downs of its maritime trade, until the creation of the port of St-Nazaire and the dredging of the Loire estuary enabled it to expand its industrial activities. Nantes is now the economic metropolis of western France.

Nantes was Brittany's first capital in the 10th century, but throughout the Middle Ages it was in bitter competition with Rennes for the privilege. The city's golden age came in the 15th century, when both the cathedral and the castle were built by the dukes of Brittany. Nantes finally conceded its rival's supremacy when the Breton parliament based itself in Rennes after the Act of Union with France was signed in 1532. It was briefly the focus of attention again in 1598, when Henri IV signed the famous Edict of Nantes establishing religious freedom throughout the kingdom.

No longer a seat of political power, Nantes achieved economic supremacy through the sugar and slave trade. The abolition of the slave trade, the turbulence of the Revolution and a drop in the import of sugar cane put an end to this prosperity, and Nantes had to turn to industrial activities,

Nantes

acquiring a new port at the entrance of the Loire estuary that could accommodate large ships.

The various stages of the town's development are still apparent today. The 19th-century district is separated from the medieval town by the cours des 50 Otages (one of modern Nantes' main arteries), while south of the cours Franklin-Roosevelt the Île Feydeau is an enclave of 18th-century elegance at the heart of the city. Striking modern buildings near the river form part of an ambitious town-planning programme and testify to Nantes' new vitality. (For a tour of the medieval town, *see pp134–5*.)

Medieval architecture of Nantes

Château des Ducs de Bretagne

Built in the 15th century by Duke François II and his daughter Anne on the banks of the Loire, the castle received many distinguished guests. After being used as a garrison for 200 years, it has found a new cultural vocation as a museum complex.

Surrounded by thick walls and a moat, four buildings dating from different periods face the inner courtyard. The two original ones are the dukes' living quarters, known as the Grand Logis and the Grand Gouvernement or Official Palace (the latter now houses a Musée Régional des Arts Populaires containing typical Breton furniture, costumes and crafts). The Petit Gouvernement is Renaissance in style, and the largest building, called Harnachement, dates from the 18th

century; it houses the Musée des Salorges, devoted primarily to the town's maritime history.

1 place Marc Elder. Tel: 02 40 41 56 56; www.chateau-nantes.fr. Open: daily 10am–7pm (9am–8pm in the summer). Closed: 1 Jan, 1 May, 1 Nov & 25 Dec. The museum closes earlier than the castle site. Admission charge (free on Sun).

Nantes is 385km (239 miles) southwest of Paris on the A11 motorway, 108km (67 miles) south of Rennes on the N137 dual carriageway. It is 2 hours from Paris by TGV (fast train). The Nantes/Atlantique International Airport, 10km (6 miles) to the south, is directly linked to Paris, London and other major European cities.

Office de Tourisme: *place Saint Pierre. Tel: 02 40 20 60 00; www.nantes-tourism.com. Open: daily 10am–1pm & 2–6pm.*

Île Feydeau

This boat-shaped piece of land was still an island in the River Loire when a series of beautiful stone residences were built on it by the city's wealthiest merchants during the 18th century. The façades are decorated with *mascarons* (stone masks, often of mythological characters) and with corbelled balconies. Walk along the Allée de Turenne and admire Nos 3, 8, 9, 10, 11 and 13, then rue Kervégan where Nos 9, 18 and 30 are particularly interesting, and finally Allée Duguay-Trouin, to see Nos 8, 9, 10, 15 and 16.

Fountain in the centre of place Royale

Musée des Beaux-Arts

This is one of France's main regional fine arts museums, with collections covering seven centuries of international art. The major European schools are represented with masterpieces by Tintoretto, Rubens, Georges de la Tour, Watteau and others. The rich collection of French 19th-century paintings includes works by Delacroix, Courbet and Corot, while 20th-century art is represented by Monet, Max Ernst, Chagall, Kandinsky, Picasso and Tinguely.

10 rue Georges Clemenceau. Tel: 02 51 17 45 00; www.nantes-tourisme.com. Open: Wed–Mon 10am–6pm (8pm Thur). Closed: Tue. Admission charge (free first Sun of month & Thur evening).

Musée d'Histoire Naturelle

Considered one of the most beautiful in France, this museum has extensive collections of zoology, palaeontology, mineralogy and ethnography. An area called Espace Science Nature has been specially designed for children from 4 to 14 years old.

12 rue Voltaire. Tel: 02 40 99 26 20; www.nantes-tourisme.com. Open: 10am–6pm. Closed: Tue. Admission charge (free on Sun).

Musée Jules Verne

Devoted to the science fiction writer, born in Nantes in 1828, this museum contains mementoes as well as books, posters, photographs, and objects that illustrate the imaginary world he created.

3 rue de l'Hermitage. Tel: 02 40 69 72 52; www.nantes-tourisme.com. Open: 10am–noon & 2–6pm. Closed: Sun morning & Tue. Admission charge (free first Sun of month).

Musées Départementaux

These County Museums are housed in three neighbouring buildings: the Palais Dobrée, dating from the 19th century; the 15th-century **Manoir de la Touche**, the former country residence of the Bishops of Nantes; and a building of recent construction. Donated to the *département* by a rich shipowner, the **Musée Thomas Dobrée** contains his personal collections including rare illuminated manuscripts and books, engravings, alabaster objects, paintings, tapestries, ceramics, jewels, arms and ivories. The **Musée d'Archéologie Régionale** presents regional prehistory and history up to the Renaissance period, illustrated mainly through local archaeological finds.

18 rue Voltaire. Tel: 02 40 71 03 50; www.nantes-tourisme.com. Open: Tue–Fri 1.30–5.30pm, Sat & Sun 2.30–5.30pm. Closed: Mon. Admission charge (free on Sun).

The 19th-century district

The wealth and style of an earlier era are still evident west of the cours des 50 Otages. In the centre of the place Royale stands a handsome fountain erected in 1865 depicting Nantes, the River Loire and its tributaries.

Leading off it is the rue Crébillon, a busy shopping street so popular with the locals that they have invented the verb *crébillonner* to describe their favourite pastime! Halfway down on the left is the entrance of the passage Pommeraye, an opulent triple-tiered shopping gallery created in 1843.

The regal, 18th-century Grand Théâtre stands on the place Graslin, which formed the nucleus of development at the beginning of the 19th century. To the southwest, the cours Cambronne, lined with stately residences, offers a glimpse of the Loire in the distance. On the north side of the rue Voltaire, several museums stand close to one another.

Parks and gardens

The landscaped **Jardin des Plantes** boasts camellias, magnolias and rhododendrons as well as collections of rare plants, some of them in hothouses. The **Île de Versailles** in the River Erdre has a lovely Japanese garden with picturesque rockeries and cascading streams. Northwest of the town centre, the **Parc de Procé** is a 16-hectare (40-acre) English-style park with a children's area: access is via rue de la Bastille and rue des Dervallièr.

Auray

The name of this sleepy town on the banks of the peaceful River Loch is familiar to all Bretons because of its famous historical and religious associations. The Battle of Auray –

which in 1364 ended the War of Succession, one of the bloodiest events in Brittany's history – took place just north of the city in the Marais de Kerzo.

The Bretons had mixed feelings about the outcome. They mourned the death of the French pretender, Charles de Blois, who was later canonised, and they resented the fact that Jean de Montfort won the battle with the help of the English. But de Montfort proved to be a good duke, and under his leadership Brittany entered a period of stability and prosperity. All things considered, they forgave de Montfort, especially since he commissioned the building of a chapel on the spot where his rival fell. Known as the Chartreuse

Town square, Auray

d'Auray, the church stands next to a funeral chapel built in the 19th century as a memorial to royalists and Chouans shot in 1795.

St-Goustan

Enclosed within a bend of the River Loch and linked to the rest of the town by an old stone bridge, this is a very pretty district, with its steep narrow streets lined with 15th-century houses.

From the place St-Sauveur by the bridge, walk round to the quai Benjamin-Franklin. The name is a reminder that, over 200 years ago, the famous American politician/inventor paid an unexpected visit to Auray, landing here when he came to negotiate a treaty with France against the British during the American War of Independence; look at the plaque on the wall of No 8. The promenade du Loch on the opposite bank occupies the site of the castle which was razed to the ground in 1558.

Ste-Anne-d'Auray

One of the most famous *pardons*, dedicated to the patron saint of Brittany, takes place on 26 July in this village north of Auray. It all started in 1625 when, following a revelation, a humble farmer found an ancient statue of St Anne, mother of the Virgin Mary, buried in one of his fields. A church was built almost immediately, although it was replaced by the present basilica in the 19th century.
6km (4 miles) north on the D17.

La Baule is popular for its modern salt-water cures as well as its grand beach and casino

Auray is 22km (14 miles) west of Vannes on the N165.

Baud

Lying at the heart of typical Breton countryside, in the green Blavet Valley on the edge of the Camors Forest, this small town is famous for the unusual Vénus de Quinipily. The statue's pagan origins caused it to be thrown into the River Blavet several times by Church authorities, where it became quite battered. The lord of the manor ordered a copy to be made and it is this that now stands on top of the fountain in a lovely rural setting (the original is long since lost). The place is the rendezvous of modern Druids, and with lucky timing you might catch one of their religious ceremonies.

Vénus de Quinipily, 2km (1¹/₄ miles) southwest on the D724 to Hennebont.

St-Adrien

This tiny granite village has a lovely 15th-century chapel, surrounded by fountains which are said to have healing powers.

6km (4 miles) northwest of Baud on a minor road.

Baud is 35km (22 miles) northwest of Vannes on the D779.

La Baule

At the heart of the Côte d'Amour (Love Coast), an intriguing name in itself, La Baule became a fashionable resort during the second half of the 19th century and has since acquired international fame. The beautiful beach alone is worth a detour, as very few anywhere combine so many positive features. Its 7km (4-mile) long stretch of golden sand follows the smooth curve of a well-sheltered south-facing bay, backed by splendid villas, luxury hotels and apartments, hydrotherapy centres and a casino.

Le Pouliguen and Pornichet

Adjacent to La Baule are two smaller resorts. Le Pouliguen, meaning 'small white cove' in Breton, was the first to be launched when this part of the coast was still a succession of shifting dunes. Pornichet, formerly a salt-marsh workers' village, now shares its marina with La Baule.

La Baule is 17km (11 miles) west of St-Nazaire on the D92.

Belle-Île

The largest island off the coast of Brittany (17km/11 miles long), Belle-Île is also the most beautiful and inspired even great artists like Claude Monet. During the 18th century, a few hundred Canadians settled on Belle-Île; they were of French descent and had voluntarily left their native Canada after it became a British colony.

Belle-Île was often attacked by the Dutch and English fleets and was twice occupied by the English. For a while it belonged to Nicolas Fouquet, Louis XIV's ambitious finance minister, who spared no expense in its fortification. The island's backbone is a treeless schistose plateau, cut by green valleys running down to the coast and leading to tiny beaches and natural harbours. The sheltered east coast provides numerous bathing facilities, while the west coast offers ruggedly beautiful scenery.

Belle-Île is well equipped for tourists, with several large hotels and a golf course overlooking the sea. The farming population lives in four villages and scattered hamlets.

Aiguilles de Port-Coton

This group of Atlantic coast reefs was painted 38 times by Claude Monet.

Le Palais

This small harbour centred on the northeast coast, facing the mainland, is Belle-Île's administrative and commercial centre and the gateway to the island, as the defensive citadel guarding its entrance testifies. In 1650 Fouquet had the original structure, a 16th-century castle, extended and strengthened by Vauban, Louis XIV's master of military architecture. The museum in the citadel has mementoes and works by the artists who painted here, including Monet. The citadel overlooks the picturesque town and harbour.

Locmaria

Set along the eastern edge of Belle-Île, the village has a charming church called **Notre-Dame de Boistord**, which is linked to a strange legend: when Dutch sailors felled a splendid elm growing in front of the church to replace their broken mast, the tree became all twisted and useless, and the terrified sailors ran away!

Sauzon

This seaside village has one of the most popular marinas on Brittany's south coast, and a golf course nearby.

Access by boat from Quiberon and Lorient (tel: 08 20 05 61 56; www.compagnie-oceane.fr), crossing 20–45 minutes, or by air from Lorient and Nantes (tel: 08 02 80 28 02). Office de Tourisme, Le Palais. Tel: 02 97 31 81 93; www.belle-ile.com. Open: 9am–12.30pm & 2–6pm. Closed: Sun afternoon.

Carnac

This is a pleasant, unpretentious little resort with gently shelving beaches. But Carnac is best known as the capital of prehistoric Brittany.

Megaliths

Stretching northwards from the village are dolmens (stone tombs) and about 3,000 menhirs, or standing stones, many grouped into three main *alignements*. Closest, at the end of rue Tumulus, is the Tumulus St-Michel, a chambered tomb dating from about 5000 BC. Artefacts recovered from it are in the Musée de la Prehistorie.

Rue de Courdiec leads from the village to the largest group, **Alignements du Ménec**, over 1km (²/₃ mile) long and comprising more than 1,000 standing stones. Route de Kerlescan leads on to **Alignements de Kermario**, whose more than 1,000 stones are viewed from raised walkways. A smaller group, **Alignement de Kerlescan**, lies beyond, and visitors may walk among these stones. On the way is another dolmen. Throughout the area, prehistoric stones are visible in fields and even built into stone walls enclosing farm fields.

As work progresses to protect the stones, the site may be closed. That should not deter visitors, who can see the stones clearly from public roads and paths. Skip the Archeoscope and see the museum in town instead.

Musée de la Préhistoire

The museum's collections – the third largest in Europe – cover a huge span of time from the Palaeolithic era to the early Middle Ages.
Place de la Chapelle 10.
Tel: 02 97 52 22 04;
www.museedecarnac.com.
Open: July & Aug daily 10am–6pm;
Apr–June & Sept Wed–Mon
10am–12.30pm & 2–6pm; Oct–Dec, Feb
& Mar Wed–Mon 10am–12.30pm &
2–5pm. Closed: Jan, public holidays & Tue
in Sept–Dec & Feb–June (except during
school holidays). Admission charge.

La Trinité-sur-Mer

A popular seaside resort with fine beaches and a lively marina. A lovely view from the Pont de Kerisper overlooks the harbour and river.
5km (3 miles) east of Carnac on
the D781.

Carnac is 34km (21 miles) southeast of Lorient on the D781.

The massive granite *alignements* in Carnac: so purposefully arranged, so unfathomably obscure

Megaliths

Allée Couverte, Île Grande

The astonishing concentration and variety of megaliths found in Brittany, particularly along the south coast, never cease to fascinate archaeologists, who are striving to solve the mystery of these granite monuments erected between 5000 and 2000 BC.

Deceptively simple in concept, yet with a profound visual impact, they are our only link with a civilisation about which we know very little. But as an indelible mark on the land, these are among the oldest existing examples of stone architecture, one of the first cultural achievements of Neolithic man, whose genius reached its apex with the construction of the Egyptian pyramids.

A world fit for giants

These monuments were called megaliths because they were literally 'large stones' – so large, in fact, that they entered the imaginary world of Breton legend as being the work of giants or fairies. Hence the name La Roche aux Fées, given to one of the finest passage graves in Brittany,

Alignement de Lagatjar, Crozon Peninsula

Dolmen des Pierres Plates

made up of 40 huge blocks of purple schist (*see pp43–4*).

The erection of the megaliths – weighing up to 45 tonnes – implied the use of a large workforce and, consequently, the presence of elaborate social structures able to organise this extraordinary collective enterprise.

A stone heritage

As megaliths are particularly plentiful in Brittany, the words used to designate the different types were borrowed from the Breton language during the 18th century. Menhir, for instance, comes from *men* (stone) and *hir* (long). There are more than 5,000 of these standing stones in Brittany, either isolated or in groups like the *alignements*, or the semi-circular or circular *cromlechs*. Heights and shapes vary a great deal.

Dolmens ('stone tables' in Breton) consist of large slabs mounted on upright stones. Sometimes decorated with engravings, they can be preceded by a corridor, or buried under a stone or earth mound with access through a covered passage, in which case the whole is called a tumulus. The most famous is the Tumulus de Barnenez near Morlaix.

The mystery remains

Experts have long debated the purpose of megaliths. Everyone more or less agrees that they are somehow connected with religious practices, but a lot of questions remain unanswered. For example, there is no doubt that dolmens are graves, but whose? As for menhirs, they are even more difficult to interpret. Were they landmarks? Signposts? Were they linked to some kind of astronomical study? Will they – can they – ever yield the answer to their mystery?

Table des Merchands, Locmariaquer

The busy port of Le Croisic

Le Croisic

This photogenic resort offers holiday-makers two very different beaches – the sheltered St-Goustan, and Port-Lin, exposed to the bracing ocean breeze – as well as a fishing harbour and marina situated inside the laguna near the salt marshes. Seventeenth-century houses decorated with wrought-iron balconies line the quayside, with more old houses in the vicinity of the church. For good overall views, climb the tower on top of the man-made Mont-Esprit. A scenic road follows the Côte Sauvage from Le Croisic right round to La Baule.

Océarium

A transparent tunnel leads right across the bottom of a giant tank, with fish swimming above and beside you. A room near the entrance shows a film about salt-farming in the nearby marshes.

Ave de St-Goustan. Tel: 02 40 23 02 44; www.ocearium-croisic.fr. Open: July & Aug daily 10am–7pm (closes 6pm & for lunch rest of the year). Closed: mornings mid-Nov–mid-Dec & last 3 weeks of Jan. Admission charge.

Le Croisic is 10km (6 miles) west of La Baule on the N171.

Le Faouët

You won't be able to resist the impressive covered market on the large village square. The ambience is magnetic and the restaurants and crêperies inviting. Once refreshed, you'll feel up to the aesthetic experience that awaits you when you visit the Chapelle St-Fiacre just outside the town.

Chapelle St-Fiacre

This interesting chapel is a gem of Flamboyant Gothic architecture, both outside and inside. Its originality lies in the asymmetry of the plain façade, with its elegant bell tower and two slim turrets linked by a corbelled platform. The real treat, however, awaits you inside, where you are met by the magnificent painted rood screen, an outstanding masterpiece of intricate carving illustrating the crucified Christ between the two thieves, but also many popular scenes, with angels on the nave side and animals on the choir side.

Christian and Celtic symbolism abounds: instructive biblical scenes are on the nave side, where the moon suggests the darkness of ignorance, and representations of the Seven Deadly Sins face the choir side, where the sun symbolises enlightenment and knowledge. Notice also the fine stained glass in the chancel.

2.5km (1¹/₂ miles) south on the D790.

Chapelle Ste-Barbe

The setting here is most surprising, with an elaborate 17th-century pilgrims' stairway leading down a rocky escarpment to the Flamboyant Gothic chapel. Inside, notice the stone vaulting (rare in Brittany) and the splendid Renaissance stained-glass windows.
3km (2 miles) northeast of Le Faouët.

Le Faouët is 39km (24 miles) northwest of Lorient.

Guérande

With its medieval contours, the walled town of Guérande stands on a plateau overlooking salt marshes. The *boulevard périphérique* offers a close-up view of the well-preserved fortifications dating from the 14th and 15th centuries, which include four gates leading into the town.

SALT MARSHES

From the air these shallow adjoining basins of sea water look like a huge puzzle. As the water evaporates, it leaves behind a white deposit: natural sea salt. Keep a sharp eye out and you might spot a *paludier* (salt-marsh worker) gathering the precious salt with a long traditional rake. The small white mounds, reflected in the water, are a familiar sight round Saillé, where the Maison des Paludiers illustrates the life and work of salt-marsh workers. Roadside stalls in the area sell freshly gathered salt in small bags. Guided tours of salt marshes available at 4.30pm daily in warmer months (*www.maisondespaludiers.fr*).

The most imposing is the Porte St-Michel (also called the Château, since it was the governor's official residence); it now houses an interesting local museum. Converging streets lead from the gates to the city centre and the mainly Gothic **Collégiale St-Aubin,**

Pilgrims' stairs at Chapelle Ste-Barbe

with its outside pulpit, carved capitals in the nave and 6th-century sarcophagus in a side chapel.
*Museum tel: 02 40 42 96 52.
Open: daily Apr–Sept 10am–12.30pm & 2.30–7pm; Oct 10am–noon & 2–6pm. Closed: Nov–Mar. Admission charge.*

9km (6 miles) northwest of La Baule on the D92.

Hennebont

One of the most heavily fortified river ports of the Middle Ages, Hennebont is set on the banks of the Blavet. Today, it is famous for its fishing and for its stud farm (*haras*) established in 1987. The late Gothic **Église Notre-Dame-du-Paradis** has a massive west tower with several pinnacles; it overlooks the walled town accessible through the imposing Porte Broërec. From the rampart walk there are views of the Blavet Valley.

The proud castle of Josselin has elaborate granite carvings overlooking its courtyard

Haras National d'Hennebont, rue Victor Hugo. Tel: 02 97 89 40 30; www.haras-hennebont.fr. Open: July & Aug 9am–7pm; Sept–June 9am–12.30pm, 2.30–6pm. Closed: Sat, Sun & Mon am; mid-Dec–mid-Jan.

Hennebont is 10km (6 miles) northeast of Lorient.

Josselin

The highlight of this charming little town is Brittany's most prestigious château, reflected in the still waters of the River Oust. At the foot of the castle, a small mooring welcomes visitors travelling the Nantes–Brest Canal. The nearby Pont Ste-Croix offers striking views of its tall towers. Josselin's winding cobbled streets lined with half-timbered buildings, some from the 14th century, are well worth exploring.

Château

Closely associated with the powerful Rohan family (who still own it), the castle was twice dismantled, but each time rose again. A fairy-tale mixture of military and domestic architecture set in a small park, it still has four of its original nine lofty towers; the living quarters are elaborated with carved pinnacles, gables, dormer windows and balustrades. In the former stables, the **Musée de Poupées** contains several hundred dolls and dolls' furniture from all over the world.

Josselin's half-timbered buildings

Brittany; legend says that it was built at the same time as St-Fiacre chapel, 15km (9 miles) away, with angels carrying the same tools back and forth. The elegant steeple and the graceful pinnacles contrast with the austere granite of the building. Notice the statues of the Twelve Apostles decorating the south porch. Inside are some remarkable 15th-century frescoes.
15km (9 miles) east of Le Faouët on the D782.

Tel: 02 97 22 36 45. Open: Apr–June & Sept daily 2–6pm, July–Aug daily 10am–6pm, Oct Sat & Sun 2–6pm. Closed: Nov–Mar. Admission charge.

Église Notre-Dame-du-Roncier
The late Gothic church is said to stand on the spot where, around AD 800, a farmer discovered a statue of the Virgin Mary under a bramble bush (*roncier* in French). An important *pardon* takes place in September.

Nearby
In the tiny village of **Guéhenno** stands a famous calvary dating from 1550.
11km (7 miles) southwest of Josselin on the D126 and D123.

Josselin is 40km (25 miles) northeast of Vannes on the D126.

Kernascléden
Notre-Dame de Kernascléden is one of the most beautiful churches in rural

Lorient
This town gets its name from the Far Eastern trade on which it was founded. The Compagnie des Indes has long since disappeared, but the town has developed its industry and commerce and is today France's second-largest fishing port and a major naval base. Almost entirely rebuilt since World War II, Lorient's appeal lies in the annual Festival Interceltique in August. A morning tour of the colourful, bustling fishing harbour of Kéroman is also strongly recommended. There is a daily 45-minute boat service to the Île de Groix, which has a bird sanctuary, and sandy beaches, sailing, skin-diving and horse-riding between menhirs.

Citadelle Port-Louis
Named after Louis XIII, the stark and functional-looking citadel was built by military architect Vauban for Richelieu, incorporating previous Spanish fortifications; it was later used as a

The Grand Menhir Brisé

prison. Climb on top of the walls for an overall view of the town and across to Lorient. The citadel houses several museums including the Musée de la Compagnie des Indes.
Tel: 02 97 12 10 37 or 02 97 85 56 72; www.lorient.fr. Open: May–Aug 10am–6.30pm; Sept–Apr 1.30–6pm. Closed: mid-Dec–Jan & Tue (off-season). Admission charge.

Lorient is 50km (31 miles) west of Vannes on the N165 dual carriageway.

Golfe du Morbihan

Morbihan means 'little sea' in Breton, and this is exactly what the Gulf of Morbihan is: an almost enclosed expanse of water with countless islands and a rich, unique ecosystem. At low tide, fishing and pleasure boats sit stranded on its mudflats.

The best way to explore the Gulf is by boat. If you have your own or can hire one, you will discover many small harbours and moorings along the indented coastline. If not, there are regular boat trips from Vannes, Port-Navalo, Locmariaquer and Auray.

You can also walk round the Gulf along a network of paths that hug the shore.

The islands

Three islands in the Gulf are well worth a visit. The **Île d'Arz**, reached from Vannes, has beautiful beaches, a sailing school and succulent oysters. Boats at Port-Blanc or Locmariaquer go to the **Île aux Moines**, the largest of all the islands, with its delightful cottages, dolmens across the heath and exotic plants. On the **Île de Gavrinis**, close to Larmor-Baden, there is a famous prehistoric cairn over a passage grave, a megalithic masterpiece, with its stones literally covered in carved decoration.
Gavrinis Tumulus tel: 02 97 57 19 38. Open: Apr–Oct for guided tours only (phone for times). Admission charge.

Locmariaquer

A number of megaliths can be found in and around this village situated at the entrance of the Gulf. The most interesting is the Grand Menhir Brisé, broken into four pieces, totalling over 20m (66ft) in length and weighing 350 tonnes. Nearby, the Table des Marchand is an imposing passage grave decorated with carvings.

Megaliths – N165, exit 20 to D70. Tel: 02 97 57 37 59. Open: May–Aug daily 10am–7pm; Sept–Apr 10am–12.30pm & 2–5pm. Closed: late Dec–early Jan & mornings Oct–Mar. Guided tours offered three times a day. Admission charge.

Rhuys Peninsula

This curving peninsula all but closes off the southern end of the Golfe du Morbihan. Just before you reach the narrow extremity, notice the Tumulus de Tumiac, also known as 'Caesar's Mound', because from that vantage point the Roman leader is said to have watched his (rowed) war galleys defeat the becalmed sailing fleet of the local Veneti, a battle that decided the fate of Brittany. He couldn't have chosen a better place, as the view takes in not only the Gulf but also Quiberon Bay and the islands of Houat and Hoëdic in the distance. A little further on, the seaside resort of Port-Navalo has a regular boat service across the strait to Locmariaquer.

Along the Atlantic side are the imposing ruins of the Château de Suscinio (*see p138*) and the peaceful village of St-Gildas-de-Rhuys, where for a short while the ancient monastery had Abélard as its abbot, after he was brutally castrated by the Parisian guardian of Héloïse. The old abbey church has a Romanesque chancel; St Gildas' tomb lies behind the main altar.

Parc Naturel Régional de Brière

See pp143, 146.

Ploërmel

Ploërmel lies at the heart of a varied rural area, between the Forest of Paimpont and the Landes de Lanvaux, close to the Nantes–Brest Canal and the picturesque towns of Josselin and Malestroit. During the War of Succession in 1351, the town was occupied by the English while Josselin was held by the French. As neither side was getting anywhere, it was decided that 30 knights from each side would fight it out halfway between the two towns (a column marks the place today). Josselin's knights won the epic battle, which went down in history as the Combat des Trente.

The Gothic-Renaissance **Église St-Armel** has a beautiful north porch with

Ploërmel's church portals depict scenes both sacred and secular

twin portals and lovely stained-glass windows. Nearby are some fine old houses, in particular the Maison des Marmousets in the rue de Beaumanoir, opposite the former residence of the dukes of Brittany.

46km (29 miles) northeast of Vannes on the N166.

Pontivy

Pontivy is a town with a split personality. To the north lies the medieval town, dominated by the defensive Rohan castle and its dry moat. You can admire its timber-framed houses by wandering through the narrow streets round the place du Martray and the rues du Fil, du Perroquet and du Pont.

Southwards lies the military town created by Napoleon in 1805, a pleasing mix of boulevards, administrative buildings, barracks and landscaped squares. To avoid confronting the British navy on the coast, the lower Blavet was canalised. Pontivy is a good base from which to visit the Blavet Valley to the south, near the Site de Castennec.

Château de Rohan tel: 02 97 25 12 93. Open: July & Aug daily 10.30am–7pm; June & Sept daily 10.30am–noon & 2–6pm; Oct–Nov & Feb–May Wed–Sun 10am–noon & 2–6pm. Closed: Dec & Jan. Admission charge.

Nearby

The steeple of the 15th-century **Notre-Dame de Quelven** can be spotted from afar. The imposing building stands on the village square, its tower and porch decorated with fine Gothic tracery. A statue of the Virgin and Child opens to reveal 12 panels depicting the life of Christ. Nearby there is a picturesque fountain. There is a *pardon* in August.

10km (6 miles) southwest of Pontivy on the D2.

Pontivy is 50km (31 miles) north of Vannes on the D767.

Presqu'île de Quiberon

The Quiberon Peninsula, formerly an island, is joined to the mainland by a narrow strip of sand dunes planted with pine trees. Sea and wind have shaped the land. The sheltered eastern coast is lined with beaches, while the Atlantic side is rightly known as the Côte Sauvage for the wild beauty of its cliffs, rock formations and tiny coves where bathing is strictly forbidden. Facing south, the main resort of Quiberon has a fine beach, a renowned hydrotherapy centre and a daily boat

La Roche-Bernard: the suspension bridge, built in 1960, is over 50m (164ft) above the Vilaine

Artist's dream: the grey stone of Rochefort-en-Terre framed with floral colour

service to the islands of Belle-Île, Houat and Hoëdic. At the height of the holiday season, cars crowd the D768 down the peninsula.

La Roche-Bernard

This once busy commercial port along the profitable 'salt road' is today a popular stop for pleasure boats along the Channel–Atlantic waterway. Take time to stroll along the steep, narrow streets of the old town dominating the River Vilaine and centred round the place Bouffay. The modern suspension bridge offers lovely views of the river. *43km (27 miles) southeast of Vannes on the N165.*

Rochefort-en-Terre

This small village, set on a promontory, is a gem of domestic architecture, solid 16th- and 17th-century granite houses brightened by a profusion of red geraniums everywhere: around the well, in stone troughs along the streets, and pouring over balconies. Notice the

elegant gabled façade of the church, which contains a late Gothic rood screen. All that is left of the château is the gatehouse and some outbuildings restored by a recent American owner, the painter Alfred Klots, who turned them into a museum of *objets d'art* and furniture.
Château tel: 02 97 43 31 56. Open: July & Aug daily 10am–6.30pm; June & Sept daily 2–6.30pm; Apr & May Sat & Sun 2–6.30pm. Closed: Oct–Mar. Admission charge.

Rochefort-en-Terre is 31km (19 miles) east of Vannes on the N166, D775 and D777.

St-Nazaire

Old St-Nazaire was all but obliterated by Allied bombing. The main interest for visitors is the harbour – more precisely, the terrace offering panoramic views of the harbour and the Loire estuary. The nearby museum, devoted to the history of shipbuilding, includes a tour of the submarine *Espadon*, the first French vessel to sail beneath the polar ice cap.
53km (33 miles) west of Nantes on the N165 and N171. The Espadon *is on ave St-Hubert. Tel: 08 10 88 84 44; www.saint-nazaire.tourisme.com. Open: mid-July–Aug daily 10am–7pm; Apr–mid-July & Sept daily 10am–12.30pm & 2–6pm; Oct–Mar Wed–Sun 10am–12.30pm & 2–6pm.*

Vannes *See pp136–7.*

Walk: Old Nantes

This walk explores the historic heart of the ancient capital of Brittany. Here, during the 15th century, the last dukes built two impressive monuments – the magnificent castle and the cathedral – as a symbol of their power. Five centuries later, these are still the city's most imposing landmarks.

Allow 2 hours, excluding a visit to the castle.

Start from the place St-Pierre.

1 Cathédrale St-Pierre

The finely carved portals, in true Flamboyant style, contrast with the stocky outline of the towers. Notice the statue of St Peter in the middle of the central portal. Inside, the use of white stone comes as a welcome surprise in a region where granite is common. The tall nave is in harmony with the vertical lines of the simple pillars, which merge directly into the elegant vaulting. In the south transept is the funeral monument of François II and his wife, Marguerite de Foix, a Renaissance masterpiece commissioned by their daughter, the Duchess Anne, and carved by Michel Colombe between 1502 and 1507.

Adjacent to the south side of the cathedral is the 15th-century chapterhouse known as La Psalette. *Proceed along the north side of the cathedral.*

2 Place Maréchal-Foch

On your right is the Porte St-Pierre, a handsome gatehouse that formed part of the town's fortifications. Beyond is the place Maréchal-Foch surrounded by elegant 18th-century residences and with good views of the cathedral. *Turn right into the rue Henri IV, then take the second street on the left, the rue Malherbe.*

3 Chapelle de l'Immaculée

In spite of its classical façade, this chapel was built in the 15th century by the last Duke of Brittany, François II. It stands at the centre of a picturesque old district.

Return to the rue Henri IV, cross over and walk past the castle along rue Prémion, turning left then right into rue du Château, which has two beautiful residences at Nos 3 and 14. Walk across the place du Pilori into the rue de la Marne and turn left.

4 Église Ste-Croix

The classical façade of the 17th-century church looks out of place in this district, with its narrow streets and disparate houses surviving from the Middle Ages. Look up at the belfry topped with angels sounding trumpets. Walk down the rue de la Juiverie, a reminder that this was the medieval Jewish quarter, and explore the adjacent streets where the ancient shops and guilds have given way to restaurants, crêperies and snack bars. The lovely old corbelled houses here are faced with slate.

Walk right round to the place du Bouffay.

5 Place du Bouffay

This was medieval Nantes' main square, where a market was held, money was minted and justice was rendered. At the height of the Revolution, a guillotine was the gruesome centrepiece.

Cross the square, follow the short rue du Bouffay and turn right into the rue de la Paix. Cross the rue de la Marne.

6 The Change Quarter

Just beyond the rue de la Marne lies the tiny place du Change. One of the best-preserved 15th-century houses is called the Maison des Apothicaires (Apothecaries' House). On the left is the pedestrianised rue des Halles. Continue along rue des Carmes, turn right into rue des Croissants, then left to explore rue Bossuet – No 5 is particularly interesting.

Walk right round, then turn left on the rue Fénelon and cross the rue de Strasbourg to return to the place St-Pierre.

Walk: Vannes old town

Built on a hillside overlooking the Golfe du Morbihan, Vannes became Brittany's first capital in the 9th century when the warrior chieftain Nominoë united the region's tribes to form a powerful independent state. This walk takes you intra muros *(within the walls).*

Allow 2 hours.

Start from the place de la République. Walk along the rue Le Hellec and turn left.

1 Musée d'Histoire

Housed in a large 15th-century residence known as the Château Gaillard, where the Breton parliament met in the 15th and 16th centuries, the museum contains a fine collection of objects. At the corner of the rue Noé and rue Rogue, look for the two happy faces of 'Vannes and His Wife', who have been there since the 1400s.
Château-Gaillard, 2 rue Noé. Tel: 02 97 42 59 80. Open: mid-May–Sept 10am–6pm; Oct–mid-May 1.30–6pm. Closed: Sun. Admission charge.
Turn left into the rue des Halles with its small restaurants. At the end of the street turn right.

2 Place Henri IV

This former 'goat's hill' (the name probably derives from pagan rites held here in ancient times) is a charming square surrounded by timber-framed houses dating from the 15th to the 17th centuries.

3 Cathédrale St-Pierre

The cathedral dates mainly from the 15th century. The round chapel is a rare example of Italian Renaissance style in Brittany; it contains the grave of St Vincent Ferrier, a Spanish monk who preached and died in Vannes.

4 La Cohue

The old covered market going back to the 13th century stands opposite the cathedral. Shopkeepers' stalls used to occupy the ground floor, while the old Court of Justice was housed on the first floor. Today, it is the home of the town's museums, containing a fine collection of paintings and illustrating local history.
Musée des Beaux-Arts Cohue, 9 and 15 place St-Pierre. Tel: 02 97 01 63 00;

www.mairie-vannes.fr. Open: daily mid-June–Sept 10am–6pm; mid-May–mid-June 1.30–6pm. Admission charge.
Walk along the south side of the cathedral to the Porte Prison.

5 Remparts (Town walls)

The Porte Prison is one of the original gates leading out of the old town. From the rue Francis Decker the walls can be seen rising behind brightly patterned flower gardens. The view is even better from the road in the park known as the promenade de la Garenne.
Re-enter the old town through the Porte Poterne; turn right into the rue du Rempart, then along the rue de la
Monnaie, and left down the rue des Orfèvres to the place de Valencia; St Vincent Ferrier died in No 17 in 1419. Turn left.

6 Place des Lices

This large square gets its name from the games and tournaments that were held there in 1532 to celebrate the Act of Union with France.
Cross the square and turn right.
On Wednesday and Saturday mornings, a market is held on the place du Poids Public, lined with delightful 17th- and 18th-century houses.
Continue on the rue Le Hellec to return to the place de la République.

Tour: Castles of southern Brittany

This 132km (82-mile) tour focuses on four very different castles and two ancient towns. It offers a look at the lifestyle of the dukes of Brittany and their powerful vassals, but also of the craftsmen and merchants who made up the backbone of Breton society from the 14th century onwards.

Allow a full day.

Start from Vannes, former residence of the dukes of Brittany. Drive east on the D779 for about 6km (4 miles) and turn south on the D780 towards the Presqu'île de Rhuys.

1 Château de Suscinio

This castle was once the favourite summer residence and hunting lodge of the dukes of Brittany. Built at the beginning of the 13th century, it was seized and dismantled by du Guesclin, confiscated by the King of France, and damaged during the Revolution. The restored gatehouse contains a historical museum.
Tel: 02 97 41 91 91. Open: Apr–Sept daily 10am–7pm; Oct–Mar 10am–noon & 2–6pm (5pm Nov–Mar). Closed: Wed off-season. Admission charge.
Return to the main road and bear right on the D20, then left at Surzur on the D183.

2 Château du Plessis-Josso

This is a typical Breton manor house, built in the 14th century by a member of the Duke of Brittany's household. It shows the evolution of a noble family's way of life from the feudal period to the 17th century.
Tel: 02 97 43 16 16. Open: July & Aug 2–6.30pm; out of season ring for information. Admission charge.
Drive on and turn right on the D7.

3 Questembert

The old town nestles round the fine 16th-century *halles* (covered market), a reminder of the cloth trade that brought prosperity. Notice the fine granite houses, including the Hôtel de Belmont, now the tourist office. Down the rue St-Michel, you can see carved on a turret a couple of figures nicknamed *Questembert et sa femme* (Questembert and his wife).
Continue on the D777 and at Rochefort-en-Terre (see p133), turn left on the D774.

4 Malestroit

It was here that a truce was signed between the French and English kings

during the Hundred Years' War.
The Chapelle de la Madeleine, where it took place, is now in ruins. Around the church are half-timbered houses from the 15th to 17th centuries.
Drive north on the D764.

5 Château du Crévy

Built in the 14th century but remodelled several times since then, this manor house is now home to the Musée du Costume with its collection of costumes covering the period from the 18th century to the present day.

Tel: 02 97 74 91 95. Open: July & Aug daily 10am–6pm; Sept–June by arrangement. Admission charge.
Drive southwest on the N166.

6 Forteresse de Largoët

These splendid ruins include one of the tallest keeps in France. In summer it is the romantic setting for a *son et lumière* show based on the story of Tristan and Isolde.
Tel: 02 97 53 35 96. Open: June–Sept 10.30am–6.30pm. Closed: Tue in June & Sept. Return to Vannes on the N166.

Getting away from it all

Everyone dreams of getting away from it all at one time or another, and there are many different ways to realise that dream. But most of us agree on certain essential ingredients: peace and quiet – even solitude – freedom, space and, most important of all, unspoilt nature. Brittany has more than its fair share of all these, if you know where to look, and the variety of its natural environment means there's something to suit every taste.

In Brittany you can glide along a canal or sail on foamy waves; you can lose yourself in birdwatching, listen for Merlin's harp, or look for elves under huge boulders in the ancient forests of Celtic legend; you can feel at peace with the world in the mellow English-style park of a great castle; or you can walk along the cobbled streets of Brittany's medieval towns.

BIRD SANCTUARIES AND ISLAND TRIPS

The coastline of Brittany and its offshore islands provide sanctuaries for a variety of seabirds, both resident and migrating (*see pp144–5*). The places listed below are just a sampling of the region's bird reserves.

Côtes d'Armor
Les Sept Îles This group of islands has the only colony of gannets in France (9,000 pairs), as well as puffins, guillemots and cormorants. Boat trips from Perros-Guirec, Trégastel and Port-Blanc (*tel: 02 96 91 10 00; www.cotesdarmor.com*).

Just a few kilometres south, in Pleumeur Bodou, an information centre about the Sept Îles has a direct live video link enabling amateurs to watch the birds closely (*tel: 02 96 91 91 40*).

Finistère
Îles des Glénan The island of St-Nicolas is an important nesting ground that also boasts the *narcisse des Glénan*, a unique species of narcissus. Boat trips from Bénodet, Concarneau, Loctudy: Vedettes de l'Odet, Bénodet (*tel: 02 98 57 00 58*).

Molène This archipelago is mostly known for its grey seals and dolphins. Boat trips from Le Conquet: Compagnie Penn-ar-Bed (*tel: 02 98 80 80 80*).

Réserve de Cap Sizun The best months to observe puffins, cormorants and guillemots are May, June and July (*see p107*). Open: *daily July & Aug 10am–6pm; Apr–June 10am–noon & 2–6pm. Closed: Sept–Mar* (*tel: 02 98 70 13 53*).

Morbihan

Île de Groix The reserve is open from June to September (*tel: 02 97 86 55 97*). Information about boat trips from Compagnie Morbihannaise de Navigation, Lorient (*tel: 08 20 05 60 00*).

Belle-Île At Koh-Castell on the Côte Sauvage is one of Brittany's best colonies of seabirds. Open: July and August daily (except Monday; *tel: 02 97 31 40 15*). Direct link from Lorient or Quiberon (*see p122*).

Séné Look for signposts for the *Réserve Naturelle des Marais* from the village. Open: July and August 10am–1pm and 2–7pm and Sundays February to June (*tel: 02 97 66 92 76*).

FORESTS

Cool green forests with their rocks, ravines and quiet streams are among the most memorable features of inland Brittany.

Carnoët

Situated on the west bank of the River Laïta, between Quimperlé and Le Pouldu, this lush forest offers a network of paths for walking and riding. The Rocher Royal, near Toulfoën, commands good views of the river and the ruins of Carnoët Castle, which legend claims was the home of the local Bluebeard.

Fougères

Covering 1,600 hectares (3,954 acres) north of Fougères, this woodland is part of the ancient Forest of Scissy, strongly associated with the Druids; among the tall beech trees can be found several megaliths and Gallic ruins. There are marked footpaths and an outdoor leisure centre. Information about guided tours from tourist office in Fougères (*tel: 02 99 94 12 20*).

Gâvre

This forest of 4,500 hectares (11,120 acres) north of Blain is ideal for walking, cycling and horse-riding. Hunts sometimes take place, so you might spot one in progress.

Pointe du Raz looks out on the low-lying Île de Sein; its islanders live exclusively by fishing

Huelgoat

Huelgoat Forest, about 30km (19 miles) south of Morlaix via the D769 and D14, is scattered with huge boulders, sometimes piled in precarious-looking arrangements over which tumbles an unruly stream. It makes a delightful place to stroll and meditate. Paths follow the canal and the Rivière d'Argent (Silver River), which gets its name from the former silver mines, and lead to delightful spots with poetic names like Trou du Diable (Devil's Hole), Roche Tremblante (Trembling Rock) or Camp d'Artus, an overgrown Gallo-Roman camp where, according to legend, a fabulous treasure discovered by King Arthur is buried.

Paimpont

This is the legendary Forest of Brocéliande, one of the most mysterious Breton settings of the famous tales of King Arthur and the Knights of the Round Table.

Discover the Fontaine de Barenton, where Merlin met the enchantress Viviane; the Château de Comper, where Viviane brought up Lancelot; Merlin's grave; and the Val Sans Retour and its lake, called the Miroir des Fées (Fairies' Mirror), where Morgan the enchantress kept unfaithful lovers prisoner.
Information from Pays touristìque de Brocéliande. Tel: 02 99 06 86 07; www.broceliande-tourisme.info

FRENCH GARDENS AND ENGLISH-STYLE PARKS

Whether you prefer the symmetry and artistic composition of French gardens or the soothing, gently curving harmony of English-style parks, Brittany's castles can offer fine examples of both.

Bois Cornillé

This large park surrounding a private château combines both French and English styles with a pond, a lake, an arbour and extensive woods.
Val d'Izé, Ille-et-Vilaine. Tel: 02 99 75 04 46 (tourist office, Vitré). Open: 7 July– 8 Sept 10am–12.30pm & 2.30–7pm. Admission charge.

Caradeuc

This is Brittany's biggest park, with numerous statues, monuments and ornamental ponds among the flower beds and along the paths.
Bécherel, Ille-et-Vilaine. Tel: 02 99 66 77 76; www.becherel.com. Open: July– Sept daily noon–6pm. Admission charge.

Kerguéhennec

With woods, lawns and lakes the park provides the setting for an exhibition of contemporary art by internationally famous artists.
Bignan, Morbihan. Tel: 02 97 60 44 44; www.art-kerguehennec.com. Open: mid-Jan–mid-Dec 11am–6pm (7pm in summer). Closed: Mon.

Rosanbo

The park was beautifully redesigned in 1910 by Achille Duchêne. Note the beautiful arbours on either side of the terraces (*see p60*).

Lanvellec, Côtes d'Armor. Tel: 02 96 35 18 77. Open: July & Aug daily 11am–6pm; Apr–June & Sept daily 2–5pm; Oct Sun 2–5pm. Admission charge.

Trévarez

Situated at the heart of the Montagnes Noires, the setting seems out of a fairy tale, with a pink castle and a profusion of rhododendrons, camellias and azaleas – truly magical when in bloom. *St-Goazec, Finistère. Tel: 02 98 26 82 79; www.trevarez.com. Open: July & Aug daily 11am–6.30pm; Mar & Oct–mid-Nov Wed, Sat & Sun 2–5.30pm; Apr–June & Sept daily 1–6pm; mid-Nov–mid-Jan daily 1.30–6.30pm. Closed: mid-Jan–Feb. Admission charge.*

Huelgoat Forest, with its mossy rocks and cool streams, is truly fit for fairies and legends

PARC NATUREL RÉGIONAL D'ARMORIQUE

Sweeping right across Finistère from the Monts d'Arrée through the Crozon Peninsula to the islands of Sein and Ouessant, this conservation area encompasses 172,000 hectares (425,006 acres). Its purpose is threefold: to protect a unique environment, to allow the scientific study of that environment and to serve as an open-air museum of nature.

The Ménez-Meur estate in the Monts d'Arrée houses the park's information centre (Hanvec, *tel: 02 98 68 81 71*), a game reserve and the Breton Horse Museum (*open: June–Sept 10.30am–7pm*). Also in the Monts d'Arrée is the ancient village of Moulins de Kerouat, built round a waterfall, complete with water mills and a tannery.

There are the Rural School Museum (Trégarvan, off the D60 along the Aulne estuary), the Museum of Game and Hunting (Scrignac, on the D42 north of Huelgoat), many fascinating places such as the Yeun Elez (a marshland area rich in wildlife) north of Réservoir de St-Michel, and the valley of the Elorn (one of the finest salmon rivers in France), as well as Roc Trévezel (accessible from the D758), at 384m (1,260ft) the highest peak of the Monts d'Arrée.

PARC NATUREL RÉGIONAL DE BRIÈRE

This extensive marshland, situated a few kilometres inland from La Baule, is criss-crossed by shallow canals and (*cont on p146*)

Wildlife

The shrill cry of seabirds is a familiar sound along the coast of Brittany, and in some places they are even heard over the deafening noise of crashing waves. All year, in all weathers, they circle and soar in their thousands, an essential part of the seascape. The cliffsides where the birds nest and settle at night seem absurdly overcrowded, but the different species, whether resident or migrating, seem to have reached an amicable arrangement.

Gannets have been the focus of attention in the last few years because the island of Rouzic in the Sept Îles archipelago is their only nesting ground in France. Video cameras have been set up on the cliff wall so that these birds, who are very shy, can be watched from the ornithological station on Île Grande. The gannets leave in October, but shags and black-backed gulls, who are their close neighbours, stay behind.

Water birds, on the other hand, prefer another kind of habitat such as the marshy areas of the Brière and the Golfe du Morbihan, the latter having the largest concentration of birds along the whole length of the north and west coasts of France. Brent geese travel all the way from Lapland and Siberia to spend the winter in the Gulf, in company with all sorts of wild

Great birdwatching opportunities for enthusiasts

Birds of all kinds, such as terns, find a hospitable habitat and a wealth of food in the coastal and inland regions of Brittany

ducks. There they cohabit with waders such as oystercatchers and ringed plovers.

In springtime, an extraordinary aerial ballet – of which puffins are undoubtedly the stars – takes place in the sky over Brittany, when the winter tenants depart for their summer homes in northern countries, temporarily leaving their lodgings to those who arrive from warmer climates.

Among the many inhabitants of the islands of Molène and the Sept Îles can be counted a small number of grey seals, quite endearing with their long moustaches and disarming look, who can be seen sunbathing on the rocks.

The publication *Brittany's Natural Heritage* is available from tourist offices, with details on walks through the best nature areas.

Puffins flock to Brittany in springtime

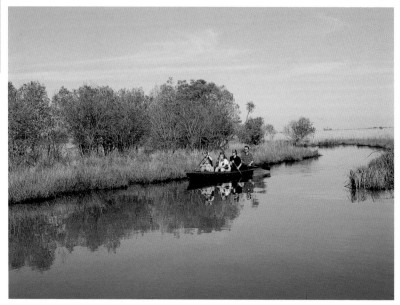

A boat tour of the Brière Regional Nature Park reveals the fascinating life of the marshland

shaded by tall reeds. Most of its 22,000 hectares (54,363 acres) has belonged to the 21 local communities since the 15th century. The inhabitants lived by farming, hunting and fishing, using peat for fuel and reeds for roofing.

Today, most of the residents work in the neighbouring towns and the marsh is gaining ground. The long flat boats are still the only means of transport to get across; organised boat trips are available (information from Office de Tourisme de Brière, La Chapelle des Marais, *tel: 02 40 66 85 01*).

At Rozé, which was the marsh's main port, you can visit the Maison de l'Eclusier (Lock-keeper's House), which explains the geology, history, fauna and flora of the Brière. Nearby, in the

Parc Animalier (Animal Reserve), a footpath leads you to the heart of the marsh, where you can observe the behaviour of birds and other animals (*tel: 02 40 91 17 80; guided tours in July and August, 9.30am, 2.30pm and 4.30pm; admission charge*).

Nearby on the Île de Fédrun, the Maison de la Mariée shows displays of old-time wedding customs (*tel: 02 40 66 85 01; admission charge*).

On the western edge of the marsh, Kerhinet is a traditional village with charming thatched cottages authentically restored. The Chaumière des Saveurs et de l'Artisanal displays a range of local handicrafts (*tel: 02 40 61 95 24*).

PEACEFUL INLAND TOWNS

Experience the unhurried pace of life in the past by visiting centuries-old towns that have kept their character. All have special treasures for you to discover.

Bécherel

This feudal town prospered from the manufacture of linen yarn. Stately merchants' houses, particularly round the marketplace, certainly testify to its thriving past. Notice their turrets and fine gables. The Château de Caradeuc is nearby (*see p142*).

31km (19 miles) northwest of Rennes.

Châtelaudren

Once the commercial centre of the coastal strip between Paimpol and St-Brieuc, Châtelaudren used to hold lively fairs and markets. This explains the splendour of the church of Notre-Dame-du-Tertre, built in the 14th century, whose vaulting is covered with 132 painted panels of rare quality and refinement.

17km (11 miles) west of St-Brieuc.

Guerlesquin

From its days as an important market town, Guerlesquin has retained an unusually large central square. In addition to a lively weekly market, the town held 19 annual fairs, specialising in wine, linen and horses. The imposing *présidial* (a former prison) was a status symbol and now forms a pleasing group with the market and the church.

23km (14 miles) southeast of Morlaix.

Jugon-les-Lacs

A quaint charm pervades this sleepy little town built on the edge of a large lake and surrounded by woodland. The place du Martray and the Maison Sevoy, a splendid 17th-century residence, are the only reminders of the town's former importance, which worried Richelieu so much that he had the fortress razed to the ground in 1616.

21km (13 miles) west of Dinan.

Lizio

Lizio is now only a modest village but, from its past as a centre of the cloth trade, it has preserved a handsome ensemble of 17th- and 18th-century domestic architecture. Today, it hosts

Guerlesquin market square and church

Old tidal mill near St-Suliac, a forerunner of the Rance Tidal Power scheme near Dinard

Brittany's largest Fête des Artisans d'Art (Crafts Festival) in August.
32km (20 miles) northeast of Vannes.

Malestroit
See pp138–9.

Moncontour
See p76.

Questembert
See p138.

RIVERS AND CANALS

After centuries of intense commercial activity, Brittany's navigable rivers and canals, totalling 600km (373 miles), are today solely used for pleasure cruising, and the old towpaths now appear strangely deserted.

An increasing number of holidaymakers are rediscovering the pleasures of river travel, and cruising at 6 to 10km per hour (4–6 mph) has become for many a new philosophy of life, a pleasant way to counter that growing sense of anxiety that would otherwise climax with a plea to 'stop the world, I want to get off!'

Two main waterways cross Brittany from north to south and from east to west: the Channel–Atlantic Link and the Nantes–Brest Canal. The Channel–Atlantic Link between St-Malo and the Arzal Dam in the Vilaine estuary is 239km (149 miles) long, the most picturesque sections being the Rance estuary, Hédé and its 11 successive locks, and the valley of the Vilaine between Rennes and Redon. Main towns on the way are Dinan, Rennes, Redon and La Roche-Bernard.

The 360km (224-mile) long Nantes-Brest Canal has been split into two separate sections ever since the building of the Guerlédan Dam. The east section runs from Nantes to Pontivy, then down the Blavet to Lorient going through Redon, Malestroit and Josselin. The most attractive part lies between Redon and Pontivy, along the Oust Valley. The west section links Carhaix-Plouguer to Brest via the canalised River Aulne, which meanders through Châteaulin.

For detailed information contact the Comité des Canaux Bretons, Office du Tourisme, place de la République, 35600 Redon (*tel: 02 99 71 06 04*). *Tourisme Fluvial en Bretagne*, a brochure available in tourist offices, gives charges and addresses of boat-hire companies.

WATER MILLS AND OTHER MILLS

The Morbihan *département* contains a wealth of old water mills, tidal mills and windmills, along the coast and inland. Their discovery through well-planned itineraries can be a delightful way to relax by going back to a time when nature set the pace. A brochure is available from tourist offices.

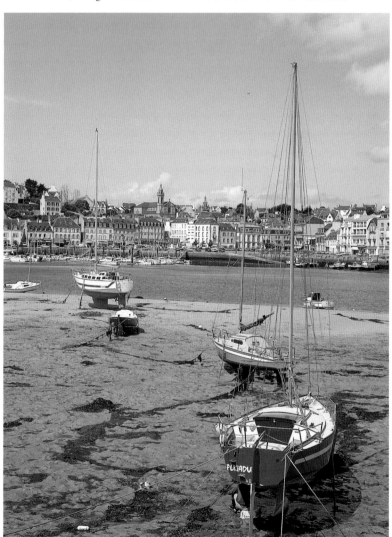

Low tide at the fishing port of Audierne

Getting away from it all

Shopping

Brittany is no longer the remote economic entity it used to be. As one of the main regions of France it has a well-balanced economy, thriving commercial activities and a wide range of shops, from vast hypermarkets to small boutiques.

Practical information

Shops stay open late in France, and Brittany is no exception. In towns they are usually open until 7pm, food shops until 8pm or even later, although they may close on Monday morning or all day Monday (this is unlikely during the high season).

Department stores are, of course, more rigid about their opening hours, which are usually 9–9.30am to 6.30–7pm. In tourist areas, souvenir and clothes shops may stay open late in the evening.

As shops accept most credit cards, there is no need to carry a lot of cash unless you're heading for a market or fair. Prices are more or less in line with those of other French regions.

Hypermarkets

Hypermarkets first appeared in France about 30 years ago, and they've been growing in number and in size ever since, gradually absorbing a huge share of the market. Located on the outskirts of most towns, they provide a Saturday outing for many families. The usually excellent cafeterias have a special children's menu, and the fare is much better than the British equivalent or fast-food restaurants (and just as cheap), including salads, fresh fruit, pastries and sundaes.

Among the most obvious advantages of hypermarkets are late closing times, low prices and the tremendous choice of goods available, from food and kitchen/dining items to electronics, clothes, garden furniture, tools, paint and even car tyres – not forgetting cheap petrol outside. There are often more than 50 checkouts, and one or two are usually reserved for customers with fewer than ten articles so they can avoid huge queues.

Some of these jumbo stores are surrounded with independent boutiques selling shoes, clothes, china and sportswear as well as services such as hairdressing, dry-cleaning and shoe repair. Altogether they form a *centre commercial* that may have one or two other restaurants besides the hypermarket's cafeteria. France has several chains of hypermarkets, though not all of them are represented in Brittany. The most common names you will see written in huge letters across the countryside in Brittany are Carrefour, Intermarché, Auchan and Leclerc – one of the best for quality and price, founded by Édouard Leclerc, a native of Landerneau in Finistère.

Supermarkets

Supermarché is the term used for a much smaller store, where little other than food is sold. These shops have existed longer than hypermarkets and are well integrated in smaller towns, usually run by local people but belonging to a regional or national chain. Prices are higher than in hypermarkets, but service – by a new generation of village grocers – is more personal.

Shopping in main towns

The most fashionable shopping centres are in Rennes, Nantes and Quimper, where elegant boutiques are further elevated by historic surroundings. Most sell luxury goods, and don't be surprised to see familiar names like Benetton, Lacoste and Hermès. Fashion boutiques, with zappy names like Energie in Concarneau and Cassidy, are also found in Rennes and Quimper.

A shopping street in the medieval town of Dinan

Markets

Colourful, sociable and lively, markets have a sense of occasion that everyone enjoys, making them a good place to meet local people (and to take photographs). Market squares everywhere suddenly take on a new dimension on market day, becoming the ideal place to dawdle and waste time (purposefully!), to listen, observe, to laugh and to marvel at life's simplicity.

Markets take place once or twice a week in towns and villages in Brittany, the particular day of the week varying from one place to the next to allow sellers a chance to attend them all.

Local farmers and itinerant sellers set up stalls of all kinds on the main square, and often in adjacent streets as well. The sophisticated ones announce themselves with bright canopies, but most of the time goods are just laid out in a jumble exposed to the morning sun.

Embroidered *sabots* for sale in Batz-sur-Mer

Vegetables of all sorts rub shoulders with beautiful flowers, T-shirts and trinkets, cutlery and gadgets, live chickens and dead ones. Special display vans offer appetising *charcuterie* and tantalising cheeses.

The background noise of voices and laughter swells to its loudest around 11.30am, then decreases as housewives tear themselves away to return home to cook the midday meal. The stallkeepers then start packing up and by 1pm the square may be deserted.

Main weekly markets

Some of these last all day.

CÔTES D'ARMOR

Châtelaudren Monday morning
Dinan Thursday morning
Guingamp Friday morning and
  Saturday all day
Jugon-les-Lacs Friday morning
Lannion Thursday morning and
  afternoon
Moncontour Monday morning
Pontrieux Monday
Quintin Tuesday
St-Brieuc Wednesday and Saturday
  morning
Tréguier Wednesday morning.

FINISTÈRE

Audierne Saturday and Wednesday
  morning for local produce
Bénodet Monday morning
Brest Friday; every morning in the
  Halles St-Louis and St-Martin
Carhaix Saturday

Brittany's renowned fruit and vegetables can be seen in all their glory in the markets

---

Châteaulin Thursday

Concarneau Monday and Friday morning

Daoulas Sunday morning

Douarnenez Monday morning

Fouesnant Friday morning

Guerlesquin Monday morning

Le Guilvinec Tuesday morning

Landerneau Tuesday and Friday morning, Saturday all day

Landivisiau Wednesday

Loctudy Tuesday morning

Morlaix Saturday

Pont-Aven Tuesday morning

Pont l'Abbé Thursday

Quimper Every day, Halle Centrale, Saturday is the largest

Quimperlé Friday

Roscoff Wednesday morning (June–Sept)

St-Pol-de-Léon Tuesday.

ILLE-ET-VILAINE

Bécherel Saturday morning

Cancale Sunday morning

Châteaugiron Thursday morning

Combourg Monday morning

Dinard Saturday morning

Dol-de-Bretagne Saturday morning

Fougères Saturday morning

Redon Monday, Friday and Saturday

Rennes Saturday morning

St-Malo Tuesday, Friday and Saturday

Vitré Monday morning; local produce on Saturday morning.

LOIRE-ATLANTIQUE

Châteaubriant Wednesday morning

Guérande Wednesday and Saturday morning

Le Croisic Tuesday, Thursday and Saturday morning under the covered market

Nantes Every morning except Monday; Wednesday, Saturday and Sunday all day.

MORBIHAN

Auray Monday, Friday and Sunday morning (one of the most important in Brittany)

Hennebont Thursday morning

Josselin Saturday morning

La Roche-Bernard Thursday morning

La Trinité-sur-Mer Tuesday and Friday

Malestroit Thursday morning

Pontivy Monday morning and afternoon

Vannes Wednesday, Saturday morning.

Specialised markets

Bécherel (Ille-et-Vilaine): *marché aux livres* (books) on the first Sunday of the month

Dinan (Côtes d'Armor): *marché aux puces* (bric-à-brac) every Wednesday in July and August, place St-Sauveur

Fougères (Ille-et-Vilaine): *marché de l'aumaillerie* (cattle) every Friday morning from 5am

Lizio (Morbihan): Fête des Artisans d'Art (handicrafts) on the second Sunday in August.

Breton specialities

Apart from the usual souvenirs, shops in every corner of Brittany offer a wealth of local products – a pleasure to look at or to take back home.

ANTIQUES

Les Aristos Broc's
Rue de Closmadeuc, Vannes.
Tel: 02 97 54 30 57.

Hénaux
25 rue St-Guillaume, St-Brieuc.
Tel: 02 96 33 07 90.

Jacques Morin
32 rue Maréchal-Foch, St-Brieuc.
Tel: 02 96 61 81 95.

Olivier Delouche
2 place Gasnier-Dupare, St-Malo.
Tel: 02 99 40 01 02.

BRETON PRODUCTS

La Biscuiterie de Quimper-Styvell
Traditional Breton lace crêpes made while you watch.
8 rue Chanoine Moreau, Quimper.
Tel: 02 98 53 10 13.

Biscuiterie La Trinitaine
Traditional Breton biscuits and food.
Saint Philibert, La Trinité-sur-Mer.
Tel: 02 97 55 02 04;
www.latrinitaine.com

Le Comptoir Celte
Traditional Breton products.
8 rue St-Vincent, Vannes.
Tel: 02 97 01 05 04.

Comptoir des Produits Bretons
Traditional objects.
3 Quai de Cornouaille, Landerneau.
Tel: 02 98 21 35 93.

Cooperative Maritime du Pays Bigouden
Traditional Breton products and handmade objects, especially on nautical themes.

Terre Plein du Port, Loctudy.
Tel: 02 98 87 41 12.

CERAMICS AND POTTERY

Faïence H B Henriot
Ceramics.
Place Bérardier, Locmaria.
Tel: 02 98 52 22 52.

Faïencerie d'Art Breton
Ceramics.
Kerdroniou, Quimper.
Tel: 02 98 52 85 28.

Fanch Griffon
Earthenware, glass and crystal.

FAÏENCE DE QUIMPER

Quimper's first ceramic workshop was founded more than 300 years ago, but today, Quimper ceramics are a mixture of styles from other parts of France, in particular, Moustiers in Provence, Nevers in central France, and Rouen in Normandy.

Later, in the 19th century, an artist decided to decorate Quimper ceramics with typical Breton scenes. In 1968, two of the original manufacturers merged to become H B Henriot, today the most famous *faïencerie*. Although it was taken over by an American firm in 1984, local artists continue to decorate and sign each piece.

4 rue Dugay-Trouin,
Douarnenez.
Tel: 02 98 92 18 17.
Gwen et Dodik
Painted ceramics.
4 rue Chateaubriand,
St-Malo.
Tel: 02 99 56 68 82.

CLOTHING
Armor Lux
Breton striped clothing.
60 bis rue Guy Autret,
Quimper. (Factory store:
21/23 rue Louison Bobet,
Quimper.)
Tel: 02 98 90 92 23.
Au Costume Breton
Traditional costumes,
lace, dolls and more.
11 rue René-Madec,
Quimper.
Tel: 02 98 95 19 11.
Le Glazik
Traditional overcoats.
9 rue du 19 Mars 1962,
Quimper.
Tel: 02 98 52 29 28.
Héoligou
Clothes, sportswear,
hand-knitted sweaters.
16 rue du Parc,
Quimper.
Tel: 02 98 95 13 29.
Kristel
Hand-knitted sweaters.
7 rue des Boucheries,
Quimper.
Tel: 02 98 95 01 92.

Butter biscuits in folkloric tins make lovely gifts

FOOD
See pp168–9.

LACE
Mercerie Guillaume
Lace, tablecloths and
doilies.
30 rue René-Madec,
Quimper.
Tel: 02 98 95 61 22.

PAPER
Moulin de Pen-Mur
Traditional paper
manufacture.

Muzillac, Morbihan.
Tel: 02 97 41 43 79.

STAINED GLASS AND CRAFTS
Christine Cocar
63 rue Maréchal-Foch,
St-Brieuc.
Tel: 02 96 60 45 72.
Verrerie de Bréhat
La Citadelle, Bréhat.
Tel: 02 96 20 09 09.

There are several fine
craft shops in Locronan
and Rochefort-en-Terre.

Entertainment

Traditions are so much a part of daily life in Brittany that they form the basis of the region's rich and varied choice of entertainment. Visitors appreciate being able to share in the spontaneous enjoyment of a people who still celebrate life as their ancestors did.

Music and dance

Inseparable as they are, music and dance make up the main, most delightful ingredient of traditional festivals. Breton music goes back to Celtic times, and some of the instruments, such as the Celtic harp, have remained unchanged.

Among all the others, the *biniou* is the best known outside Brittany; a bagpipe with one or three drones, it has a somewhat shrill tone. A *biniou* is often accompanied by a *bombarde*, a kind of oboe, this duo being the most commonly found at dance sessions. The *treujenn gaol*, on the other hand, is a type of clarinet that became popular during the 19th century and is still very much appreciated today. Two more instruments play an important role in

Traditional instruments and dances are complemented by regional costumes

Breton music, although they are by no means native: the accordion and the fiddle. Modern Breton musicians continue to import instruments of all sorts, from the didgeridoo to the electric guitar.

Breton folk songs bear the influence of medieval plainsong and Gregorian chant, and are either slow and sad or very rhythmic and joyful. Singers often accompany dancers as in the *Kan ha Diskan*, a mountain dance in which two singers in turn increase the pace of the dance to the point of frenzy.

There are many kinds of dance, multiplying into regional variations: the very rhythmic *gavotte* (also danced in other regions of France), the more fluid *bal*, and the slow *laridé*. Some of these dances are quite strenuous and require great skill, like the men-only *jabadao* and the *piler lan*.

Breton dance is not just for those performing at costumed folk festivals; it is also a popular social pastime. On weekends in the summer or near a holiday, check the windows of record shops and *crêperies* for signs advertising a '*fest-noz*', a 'night party' of live music and dance. The locals will usually be happy to teach visitors enough dance steps to make for a memorable evening. The website *www.fest-noz.net* maintains a searchable calendar (in French).

Son et lumière and historical shows

This kind of spectacle is designed to bring back to life the architectural heritage of a town or a castle through various audiovisual effects, sometimes assisted by actors in splendid costumes. Chosen themes centre on a well-known legend or on a specific period that marked the town's finest hour. The following are among the most interesting events.

Dinan (Côtes d'Armor): 'Fête des Remparts'. Medieval feast in the streets of Dinan in mid-July (*tel: 02 96 87 69 76*).

Elven (Morbihan): 'Tristan et Iseult'. *Son et lumière* show at the ruins of Largoët fortress on Friday and Saturday in July and August (*tel: 02 97 53 52 79*).

Martigne-Ferchaud (Ille-et-Vilaine): 'Les Etincelles Aquatiques Martigne-Ferchaud'. Fairies, elves and fireworks in early August (*tel: 02 99 47 83 83*).

Moncontour (Côtes d'Armor): 'Fête Médiévale'. Medieval feast in August (*tel: 02 96 73 49 57*).

Plougonvelin (Finistère): Fort de Bertheaume hosts Wednesday evening spectacles in July and August (*tel: 02 98 48 30 18*).

Quintin (Côtes d'Armor): 'Grande Féerie du 14 Juillet'. A 14 July spectacle on the lake and at the castle (*tel: 02 96 74 01 51*).

St-Gelven (Côtes d'Armor): 'Bon Repos le Pays de Conomor'. Re-enactments of great epochs of local history in mid-August (*tel: 02 96 24 05 28*).

Vannes (Morbihan): 'Fêtes Historiques'. Show and fireworks in the old town during the second week in July (*tel: 02 97 47 24 34; www.mairie-vannes.fr*).

Pardons

Pardons are the living expression of the age-old religious convictions of the Breton people. Each one is linked to a saint whose statue is kept in the local church and proudly carried at the head of the procession on the day of the *pardon*. The name refers to the *pardon* (forgiveness) that members of the congregation beg for during the religious ceremony; but it is also customary to ask for the saint's intercession or to fulfil a vow.

The procession, following a fixed itinerary, consists of a mixed crowd: parishioners in traditional costumes, bearing banners and singing hymns, plus visiting pilgrims, and curious onlookers who get drawn in by the general enthusiasm.

Mass is celebrated some time during the day, quite often outdoors, as in Ste-Anne-la-Palud near Douarnenez. The festivities that follow the religious ceremonies include dancing, eating and drinking, Breton games and fairground entertainment.

Basilique de Ste-Anne d'Auray

Among the profusion of *pardons* that take place all over Brittany, there is a distinction between ordinary *pardons*, of local interest but well worth attending if you're around because they're less crowded, and the *grands pardons*, which attract people from all over Brittany.

Ste-Anne-d'Auray in July is one of a handful of very famous *pardons* in Brittany. Like many others, it is based upon a miracle: this one occurred

Villagers of La Lorette celebrate their parish *pardon*

in 1623 when a humble farmer was shown the place where a statue of St Anne was buried. Such is also the case of the *pardon* of Notre-Dame-du-Roncier in Josselin; this time a statue of the Virgin Mary was discovered under a bramble bush. It takes place in September.

Other important *pardons* include that of St Yves, a mystic character of medieval Brittany, which takes place in Tréguier in May; the *grand pardon* of Ste-Anne-la-Palud (St Anne is the patron saint of Brittany) in Plonévez-Porzay in August, one of Brittany's most picturesque, which includes a night procession with torches; and the *grand pardon* of Notre-Dame-du-Folgoët in Le Folgoët in September.

Cultural and popular events

Breton cultural life also includes artistic events, exhibitions, fairs and the quintessentially French pastime of *boules*, as well as popular events of a more general and, in some cases, international interest. The two main events of the summer take place in Rennes and Lorient.

Les Tombées de la Nuit (Nightfall) in Rennes in early July promotes all artistic forms: plays, classical music, jazz, storytelling, dance, poetry, street arts and children's shows. *Tel: 02 99 67 11 11; www.lestombeesdelanuit.com*

Le Festival Interceltique de Lorient in August is a ten-day international celebration of music, dancing and the arts from the Celtic world. *Tel: 02 97 21 24 29; www.festival-interceltique.com*

The following is a small selection of other events.

Month varies

Vitré: Festival de Jazz, concerts around town, often in the summer but sometimes earlier. Also Carnaval des Gais Lurons, carnival-style parade on Palm Sunday. *Tel: 02 99 75 02 25; www.mairie-vitre.com*

May

Quimper: Mai Photographies, various exhibitions of photographs by French and international artists. *Tel: 02 98 53 04 05; http://mai.photographies.free.fr*

St-Malo: Etonnants Voyageurs, international book and film fair. *Tel: 02 99 31 05 74; www.etonnants-voyageurs.net*

June

Nantes: Printemps des Arts, Baroque music, singing and dancing. *Tel: 02 40 20 03 00; www.printemps-des-arts.com*

July

Dinan: Rencontres Internationales de Harpe Celtique, concerts, exhibitions and competitions. *Tel: 02 96 87 36 69; www.harpe-celtique.com*

Douarnenez: Fêtes Maritimes, flotilla, spectacles, exhibits and concerts. *Tel: 02 98 92 29 29.*

Moncontour: Les Mardivertissants (free concerts on Tuesday). *Tel: 02 96 73 49 57; www.pays-moncontour.com*

Vannes: Jazz à Vannes, major jazz festival. *Tel: 02 97 01 62 44; www.mairie-vannes.fr*

Brittany's numerous festivals draw thousands of visitors each year

July–August

Concarneau: Free music, dance and dramatic performances periodically at the Carre des Larrons.
Tel: 02 98 50 38 68;
www.ville-concarneau.fr

Morlaix: Les Arts dans la Rue, festival of street arts with music, new circus, open-air theatre and improvised performances. *Tel: 02 98 62 14 94.*

Pontivy: Festival de Musique de Pontivy, classical music featuring international artists and orchestras.
Tel: 02 97 25 04 10.

Redon: Les Nocturiales, Baroque music and Gregorian chants in the abbey.
Tel: 02 99 71 06 04.

St-Malo: Festival International de Musique Sacrée, festival of sacred music in the cathedral. *Tel: 02 99 56 05 38.*

St-Malo: La Route du Rock, most important rock festival in Brittany.
Tel: 02 99 54 01 11;
www.laroutedurock.com

August

Guérande: Académie Internationale de Musique de Guérande, introduction to music, masterclasses, concerts.
Tel: 02 40 24 96 71.

Quimper: Semaines Musicales, concerts in various prestigious venues. *Tel: 02 98 95 32 43;*
www.semaines-musicales-quimper.org

Autumn

Dinard: British Film Festival (October).
Tel: 02 99 88 19 04; www.festivaldufilm-dinard.com

Nantes: Rendez-vous de l'Erdre (September), free concerts and shows on the banks of the River Erdre. *Tel: 02 51 82 37 70; www.rendezvouserdre.com*

St-Malo: Quai des Bulles (November), strip cartoon festival. *Tel: 02 99 40 39 63; www.quaidesbulles.com*

Nightlife

Brittany also offers the sort of nightlife you find in other modern cities. Small towns of around 3,000 inhabitants – such as Binic, Quintin and Roscoff – have at least one cinema and several bars with snooker and billiards facilities. Larger towns with a population around 10,000, such as Landerneau, have one or more nightclubs.

The choice grows with the size of the city; for instance, Douarnenez has two cinemas and six nightclubs. The main towns are even better provided. Information is available from tourist offices. If your holiday is spent in a village, the local tourist office will give you a list of local *animations* (entertainment), including bingo and dancing, usually held in the village hall.

Casinos

Roulette, *boule* and blackjack are standard offerings in casinos, and also at bars, restaurants and clubs, depending on the size of the premises.

With the exception of La Baule and Bénodet, most of Brittany's casinos are on the north coast – in St-Malo, Dinard, Sables-d'Or-les-Pins, Le Val-André, St-Quay-Portrieux and Perros-Guirec.

Children

With its gently invigorating climate, ideal for the very young, and its wealth of outdoor activities, Brittany is a children's paradise.

Beaches

The most popular seaside resorts have as many as five beaches, and always one that is just right for children: sheltered, shallow, free of dangerous currents and breakers. Among the safest beaches are those at Carantec, Fouesnant, Perros-Guirec, Le Val-André, St-Quay-Portrieux and Carnac-Plage, many of them equipped with beach clubs where children can join in supervised activities and enjoy themselves while you relax.

A related favourite activity must wait until the tide goes out: looking for cockles in muddy sand, watching for scurrying creatures as feet or fingers disturb tide pools, finding unusual rocks, shells and crab claws. All they need is a bucket and they're off on a real treasure hunt!

Water and leisure parks

Water seems to have unlimited appeal for children, and even inland there are many leisure parks where children can enjoy watery pursuits along with other outdoor activities. Phone for timings.

Les Aquatides

Every variety of aqua-fun.
Les Livaudières (Loudeac). Tel: 02 96 66 14 40; www.centrebretagne.com.
Open: hours vary.

Armoripark

Aqualand, skating rink, pedalos, mini-golf.
Bégard, northwest of Guingamp, Côtes d'Armor. Tel: 02 96 45 36 36; www.armoripark.com.
Open: Apr–Sept Wed, Sat & Sun 11am–6pm (daily to 7pm July & Aug).
Admission charge.

Bretagne Pêche Loisirs

Four fishing lakes, mini-golf.
Bains sur Oust, near Redon, Ille-et-Vilaine. Tel: 02 99 91 78 78.
Open: May–Oct 7am–7pm.
Closed: Tue. Admission charge.

Cobac Parc

Water slides, ponies, roundabouts.
Lanhélin near Combourg, Ille-et-Vilaine. Tel: 02 99 73 80 16; www.cobac-parc.com.

Open: June–Aug daily 11am–6.30pm;
May & Sept Wed, Sat & Sun.
Admission charge.

Zoos
Branféré
Exotic animals and birds.
Northwest of La Roche-Bernard,
Morbihan. Tel: 02 97 42 94 66;
www.branfere.com.
Open: daily July & Aug 10am–6pm;
Apr–June & Sept 10am–5pm; winter
1.30–4pm. Closed: mid-Nov–early Feb.
Admission charge.

Domaine de la Bourbansais
Children's games; château tours.
Between Rennes and St-Malo, off
Hwy 137. Tel: 02 99 69 40 07;
www.labourbansais.com.
Open: daily Apr–Sept 10am–7pm;
Oct–Mar 2–6pm.
Admission charge.

Museums
Aquarium Marin de Trégastel
Trégastel. Tel: 02 96 23 48 58.
Open: May–Sept daily 10am–6pm (later
July & Aug); Oct–Dec Tue–Sun 2–6pm.
Closed: Mon in winter, mid-Nov–mid-
Dec inclusive. Admission charge.

Grand Aquarium
St-Malo (see p53).

Musée de Poupées (Dolls' Museum)
Josselin (see p128). Tel: 02 97 22 36 45.
Open: daily mid-July–Aug 10am–6pm;
Apr–mid-July & Sept–Oct 2–6pm.
Admission charge.

Océanopolis (European Sea Centre)
Brest (see p88).

Océarium
Le Croisic (see p126).

Planétarium
8 rue des Acadiens, Nantes.
Tel: 02 40 73 99 23; www.nantes.fr.
Open: shows Mon–Fri at 10.30am,
2.15pm & 3.45pm; Sun at 3pm &
4.30pm. Closed: Sat.
Admission charge.

Planétarium de Bretagne
Pleumeur-Bodou, near Lannion.
Tel: 02 96 15 80 30;
www.planetarium-bretagne.fr
(check for timings).

Open-air museums
Musée du Bateau (Boat Museum)
Douarnenez. Newly renovated open-air
section of the Port-Musée (see p94).

Parc de la Préhistoire (Prehistoric Park)
Thirty life-size scenes of man, beast and
dinosaur in a wooded setting.
Malansac, near Rochefort-en-Terre.
Tel: 02 97 43 34 17;
www.prehistoire.com.
Open: Apr–mid-Oct daily
10am–7.30pm; mid-Oct–mid-Nov Sun
1.30–6pm. Admission charge.

Le Village Gaulois (Gallic Village)
Visitors to this realistic 'living history'
park learn about the daily life of the
ancient Gauls.
Pleumeur-Bodou, near Lannion.
Tel: 02 96 91 83 95;
http://levillagegaulois.free.fr.
Open: Apr–June 2–6pm; July &
Aug 10.30am–7pm; Sept 2–6pm.
Admission charge.

Sport and leisure

Brittany's climate is admirably suited to outdoor sports, which make up one of the major attractions of a holiday in the region. The Comité Départemental du Tourisme (see p187), which has offices in the départements' administrative centres, suggests holiday formulas based on various sports (see Theme holidays, p176). A brochure entitled Bretagne Vacances Actives *is available from the Maison de la Bretagne in Paris or the Comité Régional du Tourisme in Rennes (see contact details below).*

WATERSPORTS

Practically every one of the many bays and estuaries along Brittany's coastline has its watersports centre. Facilities usually cover sailing, windsurfing, canoeing, water-skiing and diving.

Canoeing

This sport is practised along the coast as well as inland. Numerous clubs are there, as well as enthusiasts looking for a challenge (such as bypassing locks on the Nantes–Brest Canal).
Information available from: **Comité Régional de Bretagne de Canoë-Kayak** (Base Nautique, 35k rue J-M Huchet, 35000 Rennes; *tel: 02 23 20 30 14*).

Diving

The great variety of marine fauna and flora and the presence of archaeological sites still only partially explored make deep-sea diving all the more fascinating in Brittany. For detailed information contact **Nautisme en Bretagne**, 1 rue Kerbriant, 29200 Brest (*tel: 02 98 02 80 44; www.nautismebretagne.fr*).

Fishing

More of a hobby than a sport, fishing attracts many holidaymakers. But the need to preserve future stocks has led to certain regulations, which vary from one *département* to the next. Contact your tourist office for information about local restrictions.

If you want to make fishing the central theme of your holiday, enquire for advice and information from the **Comité Régional du Tourisme**, 1 rue Raoul Ponchon, 35000 Rennes (*tel: 02 99 28 44 30; www.tourismebretagne.com*).

Nautical events

Apart from great transatlantic races such as the Route du Rhum and the Québec–St-Malo, many nautical events take place during the season:
May: Transmanche en Double–Aber Vrac'h (cross-Channel race).

June: Morlaix–Plymouth–Morlaix; Mini Fastnet–Aber Vrac'h.
July: Cowes–Dinard; Tour du Finistère Voile (sailing round Finistère). Local regattas, windsurfing and fun board competitions also take place all along the coast every year.

Sailing and windsurfing

Wind is generously supplied in Brittany, and it's almost impossible to imagine a seascape without a sail in it. Many local sailing clubs and schools are suitable for beginners and proficient amateurs alike. If you sail your own boat, the weather forecast service to call is **Météo Marine**, *tel: 08 36 68 08 08.* General information and brochures are available from:

Comité Départemental de Voile
Maison Départementale des Sports, 13b ave de Cucillé, 35065 Rennes Cedex. Tel: 02 99 54 67 69.

Fédération Française de Voile
17 rue Henri Bocquillon, 75015 Paris. Tel: 01 40 60 37 00.
Ligue Bretagne de Voile
1 rue Kerbriant, 29200 Brest. Tel: 02 98 02 49 67; www.voile-bretagne.com
    The best sailing and watersports centre in Brittany is the **Centre Nautique des Glénans**, 8 place Philippe Vianney, 29900 Concarneau (*tel: 02 98 97 14 84; www.glenans.asso.fr*).

Swimming

In some areas bathing is not practical at low tide, so get a timetable of the tides from your hotel or local tourist office. Many beaches are equipped with lifeguard stations, and a system of flags draws your attention to possible risks. A green flag means 'Safe Bathing', an orange flag means 'Be Careful' and a red flag means 'Bathing Prohibited'.

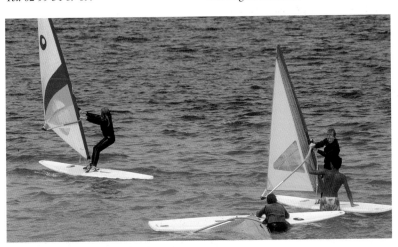

Skimming the sea on a sailboard in Camaret

Paragliding rewards the brave with exhilaration

OTHER SPORTS
Cycling

Cycling the minor roads of inland
Brittany is also one of the favourite
activities of holidaymakers. For those
who prefer riding mountain bikes,
guides describing the network of
special paths are available as for the
hiking guides below. An additional
useful address is: **Fédération Française
de Cyclotourisme** (Ligue de Bretagne),
1 rue de Vau Louis, BP12, 22001
St Brieuc Cedex 1 (*tel: 02 99 36 38 11;
www.ffct-bretagne.org*).

Flying and paragliding

There are quite a number of *áeroclubs*
(flying clubs) all over Brittany, but
fewer *clubs de parapente* (paragliding
clubs). For a list of these clubs, contact
the Comité Régional du Tourisme (*see
address on p164*) or, once in Brittany,
the local tourist office.

Golf

Once the privilege of a few, golf has
become increasingly popular in France.

Courses have sprouted all over the
country, but in Brittany they have a
special appeal because of the vast open
spaces, undulating countryside and
refreshing climate. Some courses, built
right on the edge of the ocean, offer
views reminiscent of courses in
Scotland or Ireland.

You can get detailed information on
all golf courses in Brittany in the
brochure entitled *Golfs de Bretagne*,
which is available from the Comité
Régional du Tourisme.

Issued for a period of three, four or
six days, the Green Pass Formule Golf
lets you play on any of the associated
courses as many times as you wish
during the period stated on the pass
(for more information, contact
Formule Golf, *tel: 02 40 12 55 95;
www.formule-golf.com*).

Hiking

La Bretagne à pied (Brittany on Foot)
is a series of itineraries with
accommodation suggested in the
brochure *Formules Randonnée*, available

from the Maison de la Bretagne in Paris or the Comité Régional du Tourisme in Rennes. Brittany has a dense network of marked paths, well maintained and used all year round. *Sentiers de grande randonnée* (marked GR on maps) cross the region in all directions, while *sentiers de petite randonnée* (marked PR) are short round-trip hikes up to 25km (16 miles) long.

These itineraries are described in comprehensive guides sold in some bookshops, at most tourist offices and at **France Randonnée**, 9 rue des Portes Mordelaises, 35000 Rennes (*tel: 02 99 67 42 21; open: 9.30am–noon & 2–7pm; closed: Sun*). It also publishes a free information leaflet called *Randonnée Info* and makes detailed information available for download on its website (*www.france-randonnee.fr*). In addition, each *département* publishes its own guide, free from the Comité Départemental du Tourisme (*see p187*).

Riding

If you want to spend your holiday on horseback, then you need to get the brochure *Formules Cheval*, which is available from the Comité Régional du Tourisme de Bretagne.

Alternatively, numerous riding centres throughout Brittany offer a wide choice of short and long treks for both beginners and experienced riders. Information from **La France à Cheval**, Formules Bretagne, 203 boulevard St-Germain, 75007 Paris (*tel: 01 53 63 11 53; www.france-a-cheval.com*).

During the season, several national and international horse-jumping competitions are held in Dinard, La Trinité-sur-Mer, Rennes, Fougères, Vannes and many other places. Two of the most famous stud farms in Brittany which you might like to visit are: Haras National de Hennebont, rue Victor Hugo, 56700 Hennebont (*tel: 02 97 89 40 30; see p128*); and Haras de Lamballe, place du Champ de Foire, 22405 Lamballe (*tel: 02 96 50 06 98; see p76*).

Tennis

Most holiday resorts, however small, have public tennis courts. Enquire from the local tourist office or the *mairie* (town hall).

Riding in Roc Trévezel

Food and drink

Brittany's cuisine has prospered along with the region's economy, as top-quality chefs have been drawn to its abundance of fresh seafood and agricultural products. Visitors will want to sample these creative chefs' renditions of local products, as well as some very traditional dishes found in small family-owned restaurants and crêperies.

Crêpes are perhaps Brittany's best-known speciality, but not its only one. Golden butter from Brittany is known throughout France as the sweetest, especially when made from the cream of the region's diminishing breed of *pie-noir* cows. Although Brittany is not known for its diversity of cheeses, local *chèvre* (goats') cheese will be found on menus and in markets throughout the region.

Cider is the beverage of choice (you can see it made at Musée du Cidre Bigouden in Combrit, in southern Finistère), along with the smooth and surprisingly dry mead called *chouchen*, which is distilled from honey.

Fish and seafood

Fishmongers' stalls are an unforgettable sight in Brittany, laden with rainbow harvests from the sea, rivers and mountain streams. The choice is bewildering: sole, skate, sardines, turbot, mackerel, bream, caught daily along the coast, salmon from the Aulne and Scorff rivers, trout from mountain areas and pike from the Loire.

Shellfish is also one of the great delicacies, particularly where it's served in small harbour restaurants shortly after leaving the water. Lobsters, prawns and scallops are plentiful, and Breton chefs delight in inventing new mouth-watering ways of preparing them. Oysters bred along the coast are served *nature* (plain) with a few drops of lemon juice. Cooked mussels, mainly from Mont-St-Michel Bay, are offered *marinières* (with white wine, shallots and herbs) or *à la St-Malo* (with cream).

Farm produce

The Ceinture Dorée (Gold Belt), close to the coast, produces early vegetables in great quantities: artichokes, cauliflowers, peas, cabbages, potatoes and onions. They enhance the distinctive taste of salt-meadow lamb (*pré-salé*), a local delicacy. Brittany also has an abundance of locally reared chickens and ducks, from the Rennes and Nantes areas respectively, which form the basic ingredients of some delicious recipes. Plougastel strawberries and Fouesnant cherries are renowned all over France.

The best of Breton cuisine

Restaurant menus will nearly always include a seafood starter: oysters or mussels, crab or lobster with mayonnaise, as well as a variety of other shellfish. Enjoy it with a Muscadet, a light fruity white wine from the Loire region. The *cotriade*, a traditional fish soup, is an alternative. For those who don't care for seafood, Breton *charcuterie* (cold sliced meats) are excellent.

Main dishes include the famous *homard à l'Armoricaine* (not 'l'Américaine'), lobster in a sauce of tomatoes, garlic and cognac; *gigot à la Bretonne*, lamb served with haricot beans; and *poulet au cidre*, chicken

Tiers of temptation for lovers of shellfish are displayed at restaurants along Brittany's quays

pieces cooked in cider and served with sautéed apples.

Desserts traditionally consist of *kouign-amann*, a rich cake made with lots of butter and caramelised sugar, or a lighter custardy prune flan called *far*. A small glass of *chouchen*, distilled from honey, adds the finishing touch to a traditional Breton meal.

Buying at the source

By far the best place to get a sense of the abundance and quality of Breton foods is in one of the daily markets (*see pp152–3*). Outstanding among these is Quimper's, housed in an airy new market hall in the centre of the walking area. If you possibly can, spend a Saturday morning there (the market is open 9am–2pm) browsing and sampling, perhaps gathering provisions for a picnic. You'll find the famous local butter, rows of *chèvre*, fresh-picked berries, cider and artisanal breads from Du Grain au Pain – a family bakery that really does grow its own organic grains, mill them and bake them into bread.

Several of these foods also make good souvenirs to carry home: organic tisanes and culinary herbs from Tisanes de Ker-Heol (especially their ultra-fragrant bay leaves), *kouign-amann* and – just outside the market entrance – honeys and honey-filled spice cakes. If in the midst of this, you are hungry, the market has its own *crêperie*. It's a one-stop shop for Brittany's best culinary products.

Where to eat

The French, whether at home or on holiday, enjoy dining out, so the selection of restaurants to choose from can be daunting. These fall into two categories: *crêperies* and traditional restaurants.

As their name indicates, *crêperie*s offer a complete range of *galettes* (savoury buckwheat *crêpes*) as a main dish, served with a salad if you wish, and *crêpes de froment* (sweet *crêpes*) as a dessert. Such a meal, including a bottle of cider, is quite reasonable and a great favourite with children – that's why *crêperies* are often crowded. They are also your best bet for vegetarian fare, offering meat-free options or allowing you to request the *lardons* (bacon) be left off your order.

Casual alfresco lunch outside a *crêperie*

Considering that meal times are roughly noon to 1.30pm and 7.30 to 9.30pm, it's worth booking a table at popular places. Family-owned restaurants often close for a week or two in June or July, so be sure to check before travelling any distance.

Restaurants range from the village café or the quayside restaurant to the exclusive gastronomic establishment of a fashionable resort. Bear in mind that it's usually much cheaper to choose a set-price menu than to choose the same number of à la carte courses. Moderately priced restaurants often advertise a cheap menu at lunchtime that is not available in the evening.

The star rating indicates the price of an average three-course meal in euros, including service (*service compris*) but excluding drinks.

★　　　up to €17
★★　　from €17 to €35
★★★　from €35 to €55
★★★★　over €55

St-Malo's rue Jacques-Cartier abounds with restaurants to suit all appetites

RENNES AND THE EAST

Chateaugiron

L'Aubergade ★★
A 16th-century house close to the castle; refined cuisine using local produce. Seafood a speciality.
2 bd Pierre et Julien Gourdel.
Tel: 02 99 37 41 35.

Dinan

La Caravelle ★★★
Elegant surroundings decorated with paintings; refined cuisine, poultry a speciality.
14 place Duclos.
Tel: 02 96 39 00 11.

Le Relais des Corsaires ★★★
A beautiful Renaissance house by the river; lots of atmosphere, seafood and fresh local produce.
3 rue du Quai, le Port.
Tel: 02 96 39 40 17.

Chez la Mère Pourcel ★★★★
A lovely Gothic house in the walled town; grilled artichoke cakes with *foie gras* a speciality as is *pré-salé* lamb.
3 place des Merciers.
Tel: 02 96 39 03 80.

Dol-de-Bretagne

Grand Hôtel de la Gare ★★
Wine and dine in the *belle époque* interior; specialities include a huge range of seafood, and lamb dishes.
21 ave Aristide Briand.
Tel: 02 99 48 00 44.

Hédé

Le Vieux Moulin ★★★
Romantic setting; the regional cuisine includes a special fillet of duck with honeyed apples.
Ancienne route de St-Malo.
Tel: 02 99 45 45 70.

Rennes

Crêperie des Portes Moderlaises ★
Cheery Breton blue façade frames a cosy dining room offering a wide range of mixed salads and *crêpes*.
6 rue des Portes Mordelaises.
Tel: 02 99 30 57 40.

Auberge St-Sauveur ★★
Half-timbered house in the old town; traditional cuisine, fish and shellfish.
6 rue St-Sauveur.
Tel: 02 99 79 32 56.

NORTHERN BRITTANY

Cancale

Relais Gourmande Olivier Roellinger ★★★★
In the town centre, with fresh oysters and lamb specialities.
1 rue Duguesclin.
Tel: 02 99 89 64 76.

Dinard

La Vallée ★★★
Seafood specialities.
6 ave George V.
Tel: 02 99 46 94 00.

Mûr-de-Bretagne

Auberge Grand Maison ★★★
The chef delights in pairing local land and sea products.
1 rue Léon le Cerf.
Tel: 02 96 28 51 10.

Paimpol

Crêperie de l'Abbaye de Beauport ★
Conveniently close to the ruins of the abbey.
32 rue de Beauport, Kérity Paimpol.
Tel: 02 96 20 80 21.

Ploumanac'h

Hôtel des Rochers ★★★★
Overlooking Ploumanac'h harbour

with wonderful views of the pink granite; gourmet cuisine, specialities include grilled lobster and *crêpe Nanou*. Advance booking essential.
Port de Ploumanac'h.
Tel: 02 96 91 44 49.

St-Brieuc
Le Ribeault ★
Crêperie; speciality is *crêpes flambées.*
10 rue Fardel.
Tel: 02 96 33 44 79.

St-Malo
Crêperie Solidor ★
A charming and friendly place to enjoy *crêpes* and *galettes.*
7 esplanade du Colt Menguy, Solidor.
Tel: 02 99 81 64 53.
La Corderie ★★
A very calm place with a view of the sea. Reasonable prices.
Chemin de la Corderie, St-Servan.
Tel: 02 99 81 62 38.
La Duchesse Anne ★★★
In the walled town at the foot of the ramparts; specialities are lobster and fish.
5 place Guy-la-Chambre.
Tel: 02 99 40 85 33.

St-Quay-Portrieux
Crêperie de la Plage ★★
Near the beach, open seven days a week.
7 place de la Plage.
Tel: 02 96 70 49 93.

Le Val-André
Domaine du Val ★★★
Stately mansion; specialities are *lobster à l'Armoricaine*, and home-made *foie gras.*
Planguenoual.
Tel: 02 96 32 75 40.

FINISTÈRE
Audierne
Le Bar Breton ★★
Mainly fish restaurant.
2 quai Jacques de Thézac.
Tel: 02 98 70 10 95.

Bénodet
L'Agape ★★
In Ste-Marine opposite Bénodet, cosy atmosphere; seafood a speciality.
52 rue de la Plage, Ste-Marine.
Tel: 02 98 56 32 70.
La Ferme du Letty ★★★
Close to the lagoon, with rustic décor, a warm welcome and varied cuisine.
Le Letty, Bénodet.
Tel: 02 98 57 01 27.

Concarneau
La Coquille ★★★
In the fishing harbour; interesting décor with antique furniture and paintings.
Quai du Moro.
Tel: 02 98 97 08 52.

Douarnenez
Restaurant Ty Mad ★★★
Fresh, pure cuisine in airy dining room, using local seafood and produce purchased daily.
Plage St-Jean, Treboul.
Tel: 02 98 74 00 53.

Fouesnant-Beg Meil
Thalamot ★★★
At Pointe de Beg-Meil, close to beaches, 1930s décor with paintings by Fredriksen. Specialities are fillet of duck cooked with apples and cider; seafood.
4/6 le Chemin Creux.
Tel: 02 98 94 97 38.

Pont-Aven
Moulin de Rosmadec ★★★★
A 15th-century beamed watermill on the banks of the Aven; justifiably famed food.
Pont-Aven.
Tel: 02 98 06 00 22.

Quimper

Crêperie de Locmaria ★

Route de Bénodet.

Tel: 02 98 52 06 64.

La Krampouzerie ★

Crêperie in old Quimper specialising in organic and locally grown foods – wild mushrooms, ginger caramel sauce and glorious daily specials.

Place au Beurre.

Tel: 02 98 95 13 08.

L'Ambroisie ★★★

Updated regional cuisine near the cathedral.

49 rue Elie Fréron.

Tel: 02 98 95 00 02;

www.ambroisie-quimper.com

Ste-Anne-La-Palud

Restaurant de la Plage ★★★★

Magnificent seaview and a mastery with seafood (closed Nov–Mar).

Tel: 02 98 92 50 12;

www.relaischateaux.com/laplage

St-Guenolé

Restaurant de la Mer ★★★

Near the famous rock formations; speciality is fish and seafood.

184 rue François Péron.

Tel: 02 98 58 62 22.

SOUTHERN BRITTANY

Carnac

Le Ratelier ★★

A bit worn at the edges, but perhaps the best oysters you will ever eat.

4 chemin du Douet.

Tel: 02 97 52 05 04.

Nantes

La Cigale ★★

Art Nouveau style in the centre of 19th-century Nantes. Good seafood lunches and cakes.

4 place Graslin.

Tel: 02 51 84 94 94.

La Reine Margot ★★

At the heart of old Nantes, rustic décor; traditional cooking well presented (closed Aug).

8 rue de la Juiverie.

Tel: 02 40 47 43 85.

Presqu'île de Quiberon

Le Jules Verne ★★

This charming nook with a fine view of the port focuses entirely on the sea's bounty, with daily catch options abounding.

1 blvd d'Hoedic, Port Maria.

Tel: 02 97 30 55 55.

Questembert

Le Bretagne ★★★★

Sophisticated décor; refined cuisine making exceptional use of local produce.

Rue St-Michel.

Tel: 02 97 26 11 12.

La Roche-Bernard

Auberge Bretonne ★★★

Jacques Thorel, one of the most accoladed chefs in Brittany, uses fresh produce from his own vegetable garden.

2 place du Guesclin.

Tel: 02 99 90 60 28;

www.auberge-bretonne.com

Vannes

Le Grain de Sel ★★

Updated and neo-traditional local cuisine – *andouille*, scallops and fish immaculately fresh.

13 rue des Halles.

Tel: 02 97 54 37 41.

Restaurant de Roscanvec ★★

Situated in the old pedestrian district, it offers a superb spread of traditional cuisine by a young chef.

17 rue des Halles.

Tel: 02 97 47 15 96.

Crêpes and cider

Pancakes are undoubtedly the most famous product of Breton cuisine. Now elevated to a real art, *crêpes* are celebrated every July – with the requisite music and dancing – in Gourin, in the depths of Montagnes Noires country.

What is the secret of *crêpes'* universal appeal? They are, after all, only thin pancakes – or are they? To this conundrum every Breton will give a slightly different but equally passionate response, from which one may deduce that it is all a question of know-how (due must be given to Breton pride) and of versatility (and homage paid to Breton imagination)!

There are basically two kinds of *crêpes* – or rather, *crêpe* is the name of one of the two kinds, the other

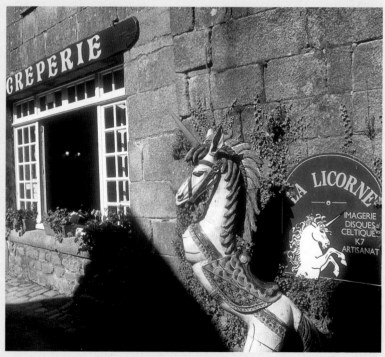

You're never far from a *crêperie* in Brittany

The cider museum in Argol

being called *galette*. The main difference is the type of flour used: *galettes* are made with buckwheat flour, an ancient cereal that had totally disappeared from Breton fields and is now making a comeback. *Crêpes*, on the other hand, are made with wheat flour. *Galettes* are served with a great variety of savoury fillings – cheese, ham, bacon, egg, seafood, onions, mushrooms, etc – while the lighter *crêpes* are enhanced by hot chocolate sauce, ice cream, Grand Marnier, honey and fruit, to name but a few mouth-watering possibilities.

You cannot fully appreciate the subtle taste of a good pancake without a *bolée de cidre* (mug of cider) or, better still, cider from Fouesnant in south Cornouaille where an apple festival is held in July. Like wine, cider varies from year to year, and there are different types according to sugar content. *Crêperies* usually give you the choice between *cidre brut*, very slightly sweet, suitable for savoury *crêpes*, and *cidre doux*, sweet and frothy with a low alcohol content, suitable for desserts.

Cider is widely used in cooking fish, seafood, poultry, meat and desserts. Distilled, it becomes a strong alcohol called *lambig* which is drunk with coffee after a meal. Cider is also used to make up cocktails; here is the recipe of a very refreshing summer drink: 1 part *sirop de framboise* (raspberry concentrate), 1 part *lambig*, 6 parts cool *cidre brut*. Cheers!

Hotels and accommodation

Accommodation of every sort is available. Simple family hotels, luxury establishments at fashionable resorts, delightful privately owned châteaux, cosy thatched cottages, rustic gîtes ruraux, friendly farms, well-appointed campsites, even functional youth hostels – you name it, Brittany has it.

Theme holidays

The choice of theme holidays is now so wide that price alone is no longer the deciding factor. More and more holidaymakers, taking suggestions from professionals, are turning to theme holiday formulas that combine a hobby or a sport with the discovery of a region, meanwhile remaining as free as they wish. Personalised planning is undertaken for you by people who know the area very well, a service particularly valuable for first-time visitors.

Among Brittany's numerous possibilities are hiking, cycling and riding tours (with or without guides) around a nature theme in remote parts of the region. Typically, detailed itineraries are provided, hotels or other accommodation booked in advance, and transport of luggage organised.

There are also sailing trips for beginners or experienced yachtsmen, along the coast or around the islands; fishing trips to the best fishing grounds in the Channel and the Atlantic; kayak trips round the Côte de Granit Rose; golf tours of the most famous golf courses; keep-fit holidays in hydrotherapy centres, and many more. For detailed information and reservations, ring **Tourisme Bretagne** (*tel: 02 99 28 44 30; www.tourisme bretagne.com*), or contact the following:

Comité Départemental du Tourisme du Loire-Atlantique, 11 rue du Château de l'Eraudière, CS 40698, 44306 Nantes Cedex. *Tel: 02 51 72 95 40; www.loire-atlantique-tourisme.com*

Formules Bretagne, Maison de la Bretagne, 8 rue de l'Arrivée, 75015 Paris. *Tel: 01 53 63 11 50.*

Comité Départemental du Tourisme du Finistère, 4 rue du 19 mars 1962, 29018 Quimper Cedex. *Tel: 02 98 76 25 64; www.finisteretourisme.com*

Comité Départemental du Tourisme (Ille-et-Vilaine), 4 rue Jean Jaurès, 35000 Rennes. *Tel: 02 99 78 47 47; www.bretagne35.com*

A sweeping drive leads to luxury accommodation in the chic seaside resort of Dinard

Comité Départemental du Tourisme des Côtes d'Armor, 7 rue St-Benoît, BP 4620, 22046 St-Brieuc. *Tel: 02 96 62 72 01; www.cotesdarmor.com*
Comité Départemental du Tourisme du Morbihan, allée Nicolas Le Blanc, 56000 Vannes. *Tel: 02 97 54 06 56; www.morbihan.com*

Hotels

Brittany's 1,000 or so hotels are famous for their warm welcome, which can be partly explained by the fact that a large number of them are family run.

Some hotels, particularly in the smaller resorts, are only open during the season, so it's well worth checking such details during the planning stage. The Comité Régional du Tourisme de Bretagne publishes a brochure entitled *Hôtels* where opening times are given, together with prices and grading.

Room-only rates, inclusive of service, are for two people sharing; but half-board (*demi-pension*) rates are per person based on two people sharing a room (*chambre*). Always check prices directly with the hotel when booking, as they're liable to change. If your heart is set on going to a highly popular resort along the coast during the high season, then you'd do well to book at least four months in advance.

Hotels are graded as follows:

4-star: luxury hotel
3-star: very comfortable hotel
2-star: good average hotel
1-star: plain but fairly comfortable hotel
RT: hotel/residence (possibility of self-catering)
SE: classified hotel without star.

Several well-known chains of hotels, such as Relais et Châteaux, Best Western and Sofitel, have establishments in Brittany.

A useful regional association that includes nearly 200 hotels/restaurants is the **Association Régionale des Logis de France CRCI**, 1 rue du Général

Guillaudot, CS 14422, 35044 Rennes
Cedex (*tel: 01 45 84 83 84; www.logis-de-france-bretagne.com*).

Châteaux

The Châteaux et Demeures de l'Ouest
are not hotels but private residences
whose owners welcome a limited
number of guests within their family
circle. A brochure entitled *Bienvenue au
Château* is available from the Comité
Régional du Tourisme de Bretagne (*see
Tourist information, p187*).

Farms and *chambres d'hôtes*

Farm holidays are increasingly popular.
Guests can have meals with the farmer
and his family, who are only too
pleased to share their love and
knowledge of the area.

Chambres d'hôtes is the French
equivalent of B & B; some places even
provide full board. Those selected by the
départements' tourist authorities for the
quality of their amenities and of their
welcome are entitled to be called *Gîtes de*

A typical Brittany *gîte*

France, and these are graded into four
categories (called *épis*), according to
certain criteria. For instance, in order to
belong to the highest categories – three
and four *épis* – rooms must have an en-
suite bathroom and toilet. Breakfast is
copious and usually includes home-
made produce.

For detailed information contact:

Gîtes de France, 42 ave du Président-
Wilson, 56400 Auray. *Tel: 02 97 56
48 12.*

Gîtes de France, 3–5 rue Félibien,
BP 93218, 44032 Nantes.
Tel: 02 51 72 95 65.

Gîtes de France-Accueil Rural,
Finistère Maison de l'Agriculture,
5 allée de Sully, 29322 Quimper Cedex.
Tel: 02 98 64 20 20.

Gîtes de France, Côtes d'Armor, 5 rue
Saint-Benoît, 22000 St-Brieuc.
Tel: 02 96 62 21 70.

The often seen sign of a farmhouse B & B

Self-catering

Total freedom and a closer contact with the local population are the main advantages of self-catering. Standards, however, vary markedly, and their assessment from a distance is difficult. Tourist authorities have therefore established a grading system called *Nids Vacances* based on well-defined, carefully checked criteria; there are one to four *nids* (nests). The Comité Régional du Tourisme de Bretagne (*see p187*) publishes a brochure called *Locations Bretagne*, which lists a selection of the main estate agents dealing with holiday rentals.

Résidences hôtelières combine the freedom of self-catering with the usual services available in hotels.

Gîtes ruraux are a category apart: country holiday houses which, like the Gîtes de France, are graded from one to four *épis*.

Camping

Apart from campsites allowed on farmland under certain conditions, all places are graded into four categories with one to four stars – and there are roughly a thousand of them in Brittany. Some top-class campsites have formed associations to draw the tourists' attention to their similar excellent amenities.

If you plan to do a lot of camping, you might consider buying a membership in the **Fédération Française de Camping-Caravaning**, which can be contacted at 78 rue de Rivoli, 75004 Paris (*tel: 01 42 72 84 08; www.ffcc.fr*). Membership is fairly inexpensive and grants discounts at affiliated campsites, as well as other benefits.

Youth hostels

Access to the 30 *auberges de jeunesse* (youth hostels) in Brittany is reserved for members of the **Fédération Unie des Auberges de Jeunesse**, 27 rue Pajol, 75018 Paris (*tel: 01 44 89 87 27; www.fuaj.org*). A new 'Pass Bretagne' offers a free night's stay after five nights in participating hotels.

Practical information is provided by the Comité Départemental de Tourisme of each *département* (*see p187 for addresses*).

Pitching a tent in St-Malo's City Fort, now a campsite

On business

Whether you're planning an individual business trip, a seminar or a conference, professional agencies at your destination can save you time and ensure that everything goes smoothly. They take care of everything: booking hotels and conference premises, planning work sessions, catering, suggesting leisure activities and receptions.

Below are names of recognised agencies (others can be found by searching for 'incoming agencies' on *www.tourismebretagne.com*):

Agri Pass

Specialists in agriculture and fishing.
29 ave Pierre Dugor, 56400 Auray.
Tel: 02 97 24 17 24; fax: 02 97 24 20 45;
www.agripass.com

Atlantica International

Specialising in group travel.
CP 30 – Le Prisme II, Parc d'Innovation de Bretagne Sud, 56038 Vannes Cedex.
Tel: 02 97 68 14 30; fax: 02 97 68 14 18;
www.atlantigroupes.com

Voyages en Bretagne

Organising conferences and seminars.
44 rue Émile Zola, 29200 Brest.
Tel: 02 98 44 41 00; fax: 02 98 43 22 95.

When planning a business trip, remember that working hours include a two-hour lunch break from noon to 2pm, during which administrative offices are closed.

Most French businessmen and women speak English, but they will appreciate your effort to greet them in French, then continue talking in English anyway if it's easier for all concerned.

Travelling

Brittany is easily accessible by fast TGV (*train à grande vitesse*) from Paris (two hours to Rennes) and by road on the A11 motorway from Paris (three hours to Rennes). There are direct flights from many European cities to the international airports of Rennes St-Jacques and Nantes Atlantique and internal flights from Dinard, St-Brieuc, Brest, Quimper and Lorient.

Within Brittany, travelling times are being steadily reduced by the gradual extension of the TGV lines and of the dual-carriageway network.

Most international car-hire companies are represented:

Nantes

Avis, Aeroport. Tel: 08 20 61 16 74;
www.avis.fr
Avis, Gare SNCF. Tel: 02 40 89 25 50;
www.avis.fr

Quimper

Europcar, 16 ave de la Libération.
Tel: 02 98 90 00 68; www.europcar.fr

Rennes

Avis, Place de la Gare. Tel: 02 23 42 14 14; www.avis.fr

St-Brieuc

Hertz, 53 rue de la Gare.
Tel: 02 96 94 25 89; www.hertz.fr

Hotels

Many hotels now specialise in welcoming business people, either individually or in groups. In addition to what you might reasonably expect,

Rennes airport, with direct flights from London

specialised hotels offer car hire, currency exchange, detailed tourist information, and transfer to and from the station or airport. Credit cards most widely accepted are Visa, American Express and Diners International.

Communications

Most business hotels will have high-speed internet access available in rooms or public areas (wireless). There may also be provision of PC terminals, telephones and fax machines, and audiovisual equipment.

Bookings

A list of hotels is available on request. Write to the **Comité Régional du Tourisme de Bretagne** (1 rue Raoul Ponchon, 35000 Rennes; *tel: 02 99 28 44 30*), or book online (*www.tourismebretagne.fr*).

Seminars and conferences

A brochure entitled *Séminaires Incentive* is available from the Comité Régional du Tourisme de Bretagne. It contains a choice of hotels with suitable facilities, as well as details on three large conference centres: the brand-new Palais du Grand Large in St-Malo, the Quartz in Brest and the Palais des Congrès in Lorient.

An interesting option is conducting seminars or business meetings aboard traditional sailing ships – an impressive and unusual way of combining business with pleasure.

Practical guide

Arriving

EU residents need only a valid passport; so do US, Canadian, Australian and New Zealand citizens who will stay no longer than three months. Longer stays require a visa. Visas are obtainable from French embassies and consulates in your own country; to be on the safe side, allow two months to receive it.

By air

Brittany is well connected by air to the rest of Europe with many airlines offering convenient low-cost flights (for example Ryanair, easyJet). There are also direct flights from Paris to Rennes, St-Brieuc, Brest, Quimper and Lorient; from London to Rennes, Brest, Lorient and Dinard (via the Channel Islands); from Cork to Brest and Quimper; from Kerry to Lorient; and from Belfast to Rennes. Nantes airport has direct links with most important European cities.

By car

At Le Mans the A11 motorway connects with the A81 to Rennes, while the A11 continues to Nantes; both cities can be reached in about three hours from Paris. A convenient network of fast dual carriageways links most Breton cities: the N12 along the north coast, the N165 along the south coast and the north–south N137 St-Malo–Rennes–Nantes.

By rail

The *Thomas Cook European Rail Timetable* is published monthly with up-to-date details of rail and shipping services throughout Europe. It is available to buy in the UK from some stations, branches of Thomas Cook, by phoning *(44) 1733 416477* or visit *www.thomascookpublishing.com*. In the USA, contact SF Travel Publications, 3959 Electric Road, Suite 155, Roanoke, VA 24018; *tel: 1 (800) 322 3834; www.travelbookstore.com*

Rennes and Nantes are two hours from Paris (Gare Montparnasse) by the fast TGV (*train à grande vitesse*). It reaches Brest, the westernmost town in Brittany, in four hours. For more information, or to book tickets, visit the website *www.voyages-sncf.com*

By sea

Brittany Ferries and Condor have regular year-round sailings to St-Malo from Portsmouth, Poole and Cork, and to Roscoff from Plymouth and Cork. Contact them at *www.brittany-ferries.com* or *www.condorferries.fr*

Children

Most hotels in holiday resorts put up extra beds for children in their parents' room on request and some offer a babysitting service. But **Gîtes de France** (*see p178*) offer more freedom and many have outdoor games, bikes, ponies and babysitters at hand.

Some restaurants advertise a special children's menu but most will make up a simple dish on request (provided the place isn't too busy) or heat up food in jars or cans that you provide. Babyfood and nappies are cheaper in hypermarkets (*see pp150–51*).

Climate
Brittany's climate is mild, with maximum temperatures between 20°C and 25°C (68–77°F) in July and August. However, the weather can be very changeable.

Conversion table
See p185.

Crime
Petty theft is a nuisance. Never leave valuables visible inside a parked car. Avoid taking money and credit cards to the beach and keep an eye on your belongings. On market days and when on busy streets during *pardons* and festivals keep an eye on your bag.

Driving
Make sure you take your car registration papers and driving licence. You must have a current insurance certificate (plus a letter of authorisation if the vehicle is not registered in your name). International Insurance Certificates (Green Cards) are not compulsory, but you are advised to apply for one if you want fully comprehensive cover. If you are not an EU citizen, contact the French embassy or consulate in your country for specific details concerning insurance and permits.

White headlights are now officially accepted. Front and rear seat belts should be worn at all times. Road signs are international and speed limits range from 50km/h (31mph) in built-up areas, unless otherwise

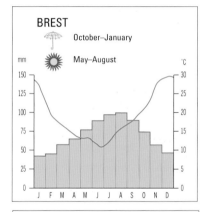

BREST
☂ October–January
☀ May–August

NANTES
☂ September–January
☀ April–August

WEATHER CONVERSION CHART

25.4mm = 1 inch
°F = 1.8 × °C + 32

indicated, to 90km/h (56mph) on ordinary roads, 110km/h (68mph) on dual carriageways and 130km/h (80mph) on motorways. Speed limits are lower by 10 to 20km/h (6 to 12mph) in wet conditions.

Traffic drives on the right. *Priorité à droite* (giving way to traffic approaching from the right) is strictly observed in built-up areas and at crossroads where right of way is not indicated (watch especially for cars coming from smaller roads), but not at roundabouts. Traffic on a roundabout has priority, so wait for a safe opportunity to enter.

Parking in town centres is often restricted; tickets are available from distributors. The local tourist office will give you a list of car-rental companies.

There are four grades of fuel: *gasoil* or *gazole* (diesel), *super* (98 octane), *sans plomb* (95 octane unleaded) and *super sans plomb* (98 octane unleaded). Petrol is cheapest at hypermarkets and dearest on motorways.

Electricity
220 volts. Electric sockets take plugs with two round pins.

Embassies
Australia 4 rue Jean Rey, 75724 Paris Cedex 15. *Tel: 01 40 59 33 00; www.france.embassy.gov.au*
Canada 35 avenue Montaigne, 75008 Paris. *Tel: 01 44 43 29 00; www.amb-canada.fr*
Ireland 12 avenue Foch, 75116 Paris. *Tel: 01 44 17 67 00; www.embassyofireland.fr*

New Zealand 7ter rue Léonard de Vinci, 75116 Paris. *Tel: 01 45 01 43 43; www.nzembassy.com/france*
UK 5 rue du Faubourg-St-Honoré, 75383 Paris. *Tel: 01 44 51 31 00; www.amb-grandebretagne.fr*
USA 2 avenue Gabriel, 75382 Paris. *Tel: 01 43 12 22 22; http://france. usembassy.gov.* There is also an American consular presence in Rennes: 30 quai Duguay-Trouin. *Tel: 02 23 44 09 60.*

Emergency telephone numbers
Ambulance (*Samu*) *15;* **Fire** (*Pompiers*) *18;* **Police** (*Police secours*) *17.*

Health
Though no mandatory vaccination requirements, it is recommended that tetanus and polio immunisation is up to date. As in most countries, AIDS is a danger. Food and water are safe.

EU residents should get a European Health Insurance Card before they travel (available free from *www.ehic.org.uk*, by phoning *0845 606 2030* or from post offices). A separate medical insurance, available from motoring organisations and travel agencies, is advisable. For non-EU residents cover varies according to their health insurance policy at home. They should get the relevant information from their own company.

Media
Newspapers
The most popular newspaper is *Ouest-France*. International newspapers are readily available.

Practical guide

CONVERSION TABLE

FROM	TO	MULTIPLY BY
Inches	Centimetres	2.54
Feet	Metres	0.3048
Yards	Metres	0.9144
Miles	Kilometres	1.6090
Acres	Hectares	0.4047
Gallons	Litres	4.5460
Ounces	Grams	28.35
Pounds	Grams	453.6
Pounds	Kilograms	0.4536
Tons	Tonnes	1.0160

To convert back, for example from centimetres to inches, divide by the number in the third column.

Television and radio

There are six channels on French television, in addition to satellite TV. Among the national radio stations, France Infos is a non-stop news programme, France Musique deals exclusively with music and France Inter is a mixed programme of entertainment. Holiday news in English is broadcast on Radio France Bretagne Ouest, on 93 FM at 10am and 5pm.

Money matters

The euro (€) is the unit of currency used in Brittany. There are seven denominations of the euro note: €5, €10, €20, €50, €100, €200 and €500; eight denominations of coins: 1 cent, 2 cents, 5 cents, 10 cents, 20 cents, 50 cents, and €1 and €2.

Currency can be exchanged in banks and in some hotels. Some shops also accept traveller's cheques. Cash dispensers outside banks accept foreign cards and give instructions in four different languages including English. You can pay by credit card or replenish cash as needed almost everywhere. Traveller's cheques denominated in euros are recommended, though cheques in US dollars are accepted in banks.

National holidays

Most places including offices and banks are closed on national holidays. Some hypermarkets and local shops stay open.

1 January New Year's Day
March/April, variable Easter Monday
May, variable Ascension Day
May, variable Whit Monday
1 May May Day
8 May Victory Day (1945)
14 July Bastille Day
15 August Feast of the Assumption
1 November All Saints' Day
11 November Armistice Day
25 December Christmas Day

Opening hours

Banks open from 9am to 4.30 or 5pm, closing on Sunday plus either Saturday or Monday, depending on market day. Shops usually open from 9am to 7pm except Sunday. Food shops often open on Sunday morning. A lot of shops close between noon and 2pm. Many are closed on Monday morning unless it's market day. Hypermarkets often stay open late one or two nights a week; they close on Sunday. Museums' opening times vary according to the season.

Organised tours

Check the brochures published by the Comité Départemental du Tourisme, which has offices in each *département*. There are more details and addresses in Theme holidays (*see p176*).

For all information contact the Comité Régional du Tourisme (*tel: 02 99 28 44 30*).

Pharmacies

Pharmacies are closed on Sunday and sometimes on Saturday afternoon. All pharmacy doors display a list of on-duty chemists, called *pharmacies de garde*.

Police

In the country, gendarmes patrol highways, while in town they control traffic, but in both cases they deal with crime as well. Check with the local *gendarmerie* for any lost property.

Post offices

Bureaux de poste are open Monday to Friday 9am–6pm, with a lunch break in small villages, and Saturday 9am–noon. Street signs near the town centre often point to the local PTT.

Post boxes are yellow. You can receive poste restante mail anywhere, as long as it is clearly addressed to you *Poste Restante*, with the name and postal code of the village or town. Stamps can also be bought in a *tabac* (tobacconist).

Public transport

Regular internal flights connect major towns and islands like Ouessant and Belle-Île. Rail links between Rennes, Nantes and other major towns are complemented by a network of coach services. The *Guide Envie*, available from the Comité Régional du Tourisme (*see p187*) or the Direction Régionale SNCF (22 boulevard Beaumont, BP 2022, 35040 Rennes Cedex), or from local tourist offices, lists all connections. Main towns offer bus and taxi services; for route plans see local tourist offices.

Senior citizens

All senior citizens are allowed a discount on entrance fees to sights and museums.

Sustainable tourism

Thomas Cook is a strong advocate of ethical and fairly traded tourism and believes that the travel experience should be as good for the places visited as it is for the people who visit them. That's why we firmly support The Travel Foundation, a charity that develops solutions to help improve and protect holiday destinations, their environment, traditions and culture. To find out what you can do to make a positive difference to the places you travel to and the people who live there, please visit *www.thetravelfoundation.org.uk*

Telephones

Some public telephones are still coin-operated, but the majority work on a *télécarte* (phonecard) of 50 or 120 units, sold at post offices and tobacconists.

To direct-dial an international call, dial *00* (wait for dial tone) + country code (**Australia** *61*, **Canada** *1*, **Ireland** *353*, **New Zealand** *64*, **UK** *44*, **USA** *1*) + area code (leave out any initial *0*) + number.

To call via the operator, dial *00* (wait for dial tone) + *33*. For reverse-charge calls, dial: **Australia** *19 00 61*, **Canada** *19 00 16*, **New Zealand** *19 00 64*, **UK** *19 00 44*, **USA** *19 00 11* and *19 00 19*.

Calls from hotels are more expensive. International calls are cheaper after 7.30pm and on Saturday and Sunday.

Time
Summer: GMT + 2; Winter: GMT + 1.

Tipping
Service charges are included in restaurants and cafés, but it is customary to tip for other services.

Toilets
There are public toilets in commercial centres, hypermarkets, petrol stations, cafés and restaurants. Smaller establishments sometimes have a single facility for both sexes.

Tourist information
National
Maison de la Bretagne, 8 rue de l'Arrivée, 75015 Paris.
Tel: 01 53 63 11 50;
www.tourisme.fr

Regional
Comité Régional du Tourisme, 1 rue Raoul Ponchon, 35000 Rennes.
Tel: 02 99 28 44 30;
www.tourismebretagne.com

Departmental
Comité Départemental du Tourisme, located at: 11 rue du Château de l'Eraudière, CS 40698, 44306 Nantes Cedex. *Tel: 02 51 72 95 40;*
www.loire-atlantique-tourisme.com
4 rue du 19 mars 1962, 29018 Quimper Cedex. *Tel: 02 98 76 25 64;*
www.finisteretourisme.com
4 rue Jean Jaurès, 35000 Rennes.
Tel: 02 99 78 47 47;
www.bretagne35.com
7 rue St-Benôit, BP 4620, 22046 St-Brieuc. *Tel: 02 96 62 72 01;*
www.cotesdarmor.com
Allée Nicolas Le Blanc, 56000 Vannes.
Tel: 02 97 54 06 56; www.morbihan.com

Local
The list of local tourist offices can be found in all information brochures.

Travellers with disabilities
For hotels and campsites see the official brochures *Guide Campings* and *Guide Hôtels* published by the Comité Régional du Tourisme de Bretagne.

The Comité Départemental du Tourisme of each *département* publishes a guide listing easily accessible sights, available on request. For more general information write to the **Association des Paralyses de France** (17 boulevard Auguste Blanqui, 75013 Paris, *tel: 01 40 78 69 00; www.apf.asso.fr*).

Language

Everyone in Brittany speaks French, and quite a few people also speak Breton.

COMMON BRETON WORDS

aber	estuary	**loc**	monastery
argoat	inland, wooded area	**menez**	mountain
armor	coastline	**meur**	large, important
beg	point	**penn**	head, tip, summit
bihan	small	**plou**	parish
bras	large	**porz**	port
Breizh	Brittany	**roc'h**	rock
castel	castle	**ros**	mound, hill
fest-noz	night feast	**ti**	house
ker	village, hamlet	**tro**	valley
lan	church		

BASIC FRENCH WORDS AND PHRASES

yes	oui	**At what time . . . ?**	A quelle heure . . .
no	non	**here**	ici
please	s'il vous plaît	**there**	là
thank you	merci	**near**	près
excuse me	excusez-moi	**before**	avant
I'm sorry	pardon	**in front of**	devant
good morning	bonjour	**behind**	derrière
good evening	bonsoir	**opposite**	en face de
goodnight	bonne nuit	**right**	à droite
goodbye	au revoir	**left**	à gauche
I have . . .	J'ai . . .	**straight on**	tout droit
It is . . .	C'est . . .	**road**	la route
Do you speak	Parlez-vous	**motorway**	l'autoroute
English?	anglais?	**dual carriageway**	la voie express
I do not understand	Je ne comprends pas	**bridge**	le pont
Could you speak	Pouvez-vous parler	**street**	la rue
more slowly	plus lentement	**garage/petrol**	la station
please?	s'il vous plaît?	**station**	service
I would like . . .	Je voudrais . . .	**My car has**	Ma voiture est
when	quand	**broken down**	en panne
yesterday	hier	**railway station**	la gare
today	aujourd'hui	**platform**	le quai
tomorrow	demain	**a ticket for . . .**	un billet pour . . .

harbour	le port	red/white	rouge/blanc
airport	l'aéroport	water	de l'eau
flight to . . .	le vol à	coffee	un café
	destination de . . .	white	au lait
I am looking	Je cherche . . .	beer	de la bière
for . . . (hotel,	(l'hôtel, le	cider	du cidre
castle, etc)	château, etc)	tea with milk	un thé au lait
to eat	manger	Waiter!	Monsieur!
to drink	boire	Waitress!	Mademoiselle!
menu	la carte	Where are	Où sont les
starters	les hors d'oeuvre	the toilets?	toilettes?
meat	la viande	Can I have	L'addition s'il
rare	saignant	the bill?	vous plaît
well done	bien cuit	shop	le magasin
fish	le poisson	market	le marché
seafood	les fruits de mer	open	ouvert
I am a vegetarian	Je suis	closed	fermé
	végétarien(ne)	money	l'argent
vegetables	les légumes	notes	des billets
chips	des frites	traveller's	des chèques
salt/pepper	du sel/poivre	cheques	de voyage
bread	du pain	How much	Combien
butter	du beurre	is this?	coûte ceci?
cheese	du fromage	May I have	Puis-je avoir
wine list	la carte des vins	a receipt?	un reçu?

NUMBERS

1	un	20	vingt
2	deux	30	trente
3	trois	40	quarante
4	quatre	50	cinquante
5	cinq	100	cent
6	six	1,000	mille
7	sept		
8	huit		
9	neuf		
10	dix		

Index

Acknowledgements

Thomas Cook wishes to thank the photographers, picture libraries and other organisations for the loan of the photographs reproduced in this book, to whom copyright belongs:

THE BRIDGEMAN ART LIBRARY 103
COMITÉ RÉGIONAL DU TOURISME DE BRETAGNE 18 (Jean Brau); 24, 88 (Jean-Patrick Gratien); 53, 58, 64, 127 (Henry Marcou); 66, 87 (George Fisher); 102 (Erich Spiegelhalter); 118 (OTNA/Guilhem Ducleon A.); 129, 130 (Anatoly Bobrovitch); 147, 158 (SELVA); 178a
DREAMSTIME.COM 1 (Elena Elisseeva)
MARY EVANS PICTURE LIBRARY 9
ERIC PARKS 12, 86
PICTURES COLOUR LIBRARY 63
ROBERT HARDING PICTURE LIBRARY 71
SPECTRUM 55, 117, 145b
STILLMAN ROGERS 144
WIKIMEDIA COMMONS 17 (Vassil)
WORLD PICTURES/PHOTOSHOT 13, 15, 120

The remaining pictures are held in the AA PHOTO LIBRARY and were taken by RICK STRANGE with the exception of pages 40, 41, 43, 44, 56, 83, 133, 159, 169 which were taken by A BAKER; pages 5, 16, 28, 30, 33, 36, 38, 39, 59, 61, 78, 148, 170a, 170b, 177, 178b, 179, 181 which were taken by STEVE DAY; pages 31, 34, 79, 155, 160, 165 which were taken by BARRIE SMITH; and pages 7, 21, 25, 68, 69, 84, 92, 143, 149, 151, 153, 166, 174 which were taken by ROY VICTOR.

For CAMBRIDGE PUBLISHING MANAGEMENT LTD:
Project editor: Tom Lee
Typesetter: Trevor Double
Proofreader: Karolin Thomas
Indexer: Karolin Thomas

SEND YOUR THOUGHTS TO
BOOKS@THOMASCOOK.COM

We're committed to providing the very best up-to-date information in our travel guides and constantly strive to make them as useful as they can be. You can help us to improve future editions by letting us have your feedback. If you've made a wonderful discovery on your travels that we don't already feature, if you'd like to inform us about recent changes to anything that we do include, or if you simply want to let us know your thoughts about this guidebook and how we can make it even better – we'd love to hear from you.

Send us ideas, discoveries and recommendations today and then look out for your valuable input in the next edition of this title.

Emails to the above address, or letters to Travellers Series Editor, Thomas Cook Publishing, PO Box 227, Unit 9, Coningsby Road, Peterborough PE3 8SB, UK.

Please don't forget to let us know which title your feedback refers to!